Contemporary Discourse
in the Field of
ASTRONOMY ™

How Mathematical Models, Computer Simulations, and Exploration Can Be Used to Study the Universe

An Anthology of Current Thought

Edited by Heather Hasan

The Rosen Publishing Group, Inc., New York

To my dad—though I'll never be as tall as you, you've always made me feel ten feet tall

Published in 2006 by The Rosen Publishing Group, Inc.
29 East 21st Street, New York, NY 10010

First Edition

Library of Congress Cataloging-in-Publication Data

How mathematical models, computer simulations, and exploration can be used to study the universe: an anthology of current thought/edited by Heather Hasan.—1st ed.
    p. cm.—(Contemporary discourse in the field of astronomy)
Includes bibliographical references and index.
ISBN 1-4042-0393-1 (lib. bdg.)
1. Astronomy—Mathematics. 2. Astronomy—Computer simulation. 3. Universe.
I. Hasan, Heather. II. Series.
QB47.H68 2005
520'.01'5118—dc22

                                                                2004027377

Manufactured in the United States of America

On the cover: Bottom right: Hubble telescope view of V838 Mon, a distant star. Bottom left: Galileo Galilei. Center left: the Dumbell Nebula. Top right: solar flares.

CONTENTS

The quest to understand lies at the heart of astronomy. Those who pursue it seek to answer questions about the past, present, and future of the universe. One cannot help but be amazed by the progress astronomers have made in a relatively short span of time. They have formed a detailed picture of Earth, our solar system, and even the galaxies of deep space. How did they do it? They did it by adhering to the scientific method—through observation, theorization, testing, and exploration.

Early astronomy involved observing and predicting the motions of the celestial objects that were visible to the naked eye. From their observations, scientists such as Aristotle, Ptolemy, Copernicus, Brahe, and Kepler developed theories and created mathematical models to explain them.

However, it is important to remember that any scientific theory is only valid until a better scientific theory comes along. When a scientific theory fails to explain present phenomena, a new theory, or at least a modification of the old theory, is needed. For instance, Sir Isaac Newton's (1642–1727) theory of gravitation accounted for the orbits of the planets around the Sun and allowed for the prediction of the ocean tides, but it wasn't a theory without flaws. One of its flaws was that the orbit of Mercury was not accurately described. Therefore, Albert Einstein (1879–1955) proposed a new theory of gravitation, which was included in his general theory of relativity. Though Newton's theory was slightly off, we still use it today to send rockets into space, to plot the orbits of comets, and to calculate the masses of galaxies millions of light-years away. Einstein's theory may be slightly off as well, but it still enables us to build nuclear power plants.

Scientific theories often have to be revised after the discovery of a revolutionary technology. This was the case 400 years ago when Galileo used the newly invented telescope to gaze upon the heavens. Since then, the field of astronomy has progressed in leaps and bounds.

The telescope has itself advanced greatly since Galileo first studied the stars with his small refracting telescope. Refracting telescopes, which use a lens to focus light onto an image, were made larger and larger, and lenses were added in attempts to see farther into space and with greater clarity. Finally, in the 1730s, the reflecting telescope, which uses concave mirrors to focus light, was invented.

Telescopes were made even more useful in the recent past. Reflecting telescopes have been made to gather light from different parts of the electromagnetic spectrum. These telescopes have made it possible to view objects that were undetectable with optical telescopes, which were only able to gather light from the visible range of the spectrum. Though most telescopes are located on Earth, we have enhanced our exploration of the universe by sending others out into space.

The development of calculus in the early seventeenth century made the calculation of changing quantities, such as the speed at which a celestial body is moving, easier and more accurate. The ability to represent geometric quantities with algebraic expressions also allowed for the refinement of existing astronomical models. The groundwork for mathematical techniques in astronomy was laid in the seventeenth century, but it did not end there. In the following centuries, more sophisticated mathematical methods were built upon the foundations of calculus and trigonometry and were applied to astronomy. Today, astronomical calculations that were once carried out using slide rules are now solved using sophisticated computer programs.

Modern astronomy has come to rely heavily on computers. Computers are used for everything from control of the telescopes to image processing and scientific analysis. They are also used to create computer simulations, or models of theoretical physical systems. Over the past twenty years or so, computer simulations have become one of the primary tools that theoreticians have at their disposal to help them understand the universe. Computer simulated universes allow astronomers to translate various assumptions about the universe into material evidence. With this technology, astronomers now have the ability to "see" the most distant parts of the universe.

Though we are not yet capable of physically traveling to the far reaches of the universe, we have been able to explore parts of our solar system through space travel. With the advent of the National Aeronautics and Space Administration (NASA) in 1958, the United States began a rich history of scientific and technological achievements in human spaceflight, space science, and space applications. With human spaceflight missions, such as Project Mercury and Project Gemini, NASA proved that humans could indeed travel in space. The Apollo program went one step further, placing man on the Moon. Skylab and the International Space Station have also demonstrated that humans can live and work in space for extended periods of time. From the space shuttle to robotic exploration of the Moon and Mars, NASA has proven that space exploration is not only possible but essential to the future of scientific discovery.

Certainly, we stand at a crossroads in the field of astronomy. As time passes, the instruments of astronomy have become more and more sophisticated, and with the increasing degree of complexity comes a larger price tag. The United States government and private corporations invest billions of dollars in space exploration and other space technologies, but for how long remains to be seen. Meanwhile, new technologies may be developed to revolutionize the study of the universe, just as the telescope revolutionized astronomy 400 years ago.

This anthology is intended to give the reader a general understanding of the science of astronomy—

and also what the future may hold. It will focus on how current technologies such as mathematical models and computer simulations are being used by astronomers to advance our understanding of the universe. It will also endeavor to show why an understanding of the universe is not just for scientists. Astronomy is more than a study of the physical universe; it's also about learning humankind's place within it. —HH

The Units of Astronomy

Measurements in astronomy rely on units that simplify the calculation of vast distances. The most common unit of measurement of distance within the solar system is the astronomical unit (AU). One AU is the average distance between Earth and the Sun, 92,960,116 miles (149,597,870 kilometers). Thus, the AU allows measurements to be recorded using relatively small numbers, rather than large, unwieldy numbers.

The transits of Venus, the passages of Venus across the face of the Sun, played a central role in the first calculations of the astronomical unit. Although Venus has moved across the face of the Sun periodically since the formation of the solar system, the first recorded description of a transit of Venus is from 1639. Five transits have occurred since then. These are the transits of 1761, 1769, 1874, 1882, and 2004. The following article from the Chronicle of Higher Education, written about one month before the June 8, 2004,

*transit of Venus, explains the history of the
astronomical unit and the use of the 1769
transit of Venus in calculating it. —HH*

"The Venus Hunters"
by Richard Monastersky
The Chronicle of Higher Education, May 14, 2004

Early next month, billions of people around the world
will have a chance to see something that nobody alive
has ever witnessed. On June 8, Venus will slowly march
across the face of the Sun—creating a small black
period that will punctuate the fiery solar disk.

The celestial event, called a transit of Venus, last
took place in 1882, when it created such a stir that spec-
tators jammed Wall Street, and global powers opened
their coffers in fits of patriotic frenzy to see which
nation could best observe the phenomenon from remote
spots on Earth.

Astronomers risked their lives, and occasionally
lost them, because they hoped to use the transit to
measure the distance between the Earth and the Sun.
That value, named the astronomical unit, once provided
the fundamental means to map the positions of heavenly bodies and determine the size of the universe. The
measurement was so central to those tasks that the
British Astronomer Royal in the mid-19th century
called it "the noblest problem in astronomy."

"At one time it was the most important thing in
astronomy," says Jay M. Pasachoff, a professor of astronomy at Williams College. Nations spent the equivalent of

millions of dollars mounting transit expeditions that pre-figured the Apollo missions and the robotic rovers now driving across the surface of Mars.

"In the 19th century it was really analogous to the space race," says Steven J. Dick, chief historian at NASA. "Any country that had a scientific reputation sent out [transit] expeditions. It was a race to see who could come up with the best technique and final answer."

Today astronomers have more accurate ways of determining the astronomical unit, but many researchers will nonetheless take up their telescopes next month to observe the transit of Venus. They will gather, in small groups and at major conferences in England and Iran, to pay homage to intellectual fore-bears who struggled so heroically to document this rare occurrence. The tales of those exploits recall some of the biggest names in science and provide snapshots of key moments in the past four centuries when astronomy intersected with wars, empires, and exploration.

Britain, for example, sent Captain James Cook off to the South Pacific to observe a transit in 1769, in a mission that eventually took on far more importance as a means of expanding the British Empire. Charles Mason and Jeremiah Dixon set off to measure the 1761 transit and so impressed their superiors that they later were assigned to survey the border between Maryland and Pennsylvania, a project that resulted in the Mason-Dixon line. And the 1882 transit made such an impression on the young John Philip Sousa that he wrote a march and later a novel about the event.

Chance of a Lifetime

Although Venus has been passing between Earth and the Sun since the dawn of the planets, history has no record of anybody witnessing the event until 1639. Even then, only two people had that honor—and they almost missed it.

Since then, Venus has transited across the Sun only four times, in 1761, 1769, 1874 and 1882. The planetary show happens so infrequently because Venus's orbit tilts slightly relative to Earth's. Roughly every 116 years the orbits line up, and Venus appears for six hours as a tiny dot migrating across the Sun's face.

If people can't catch the June 8 transit this year, they might have a chance—depending on where they live—to see the next occurrence, on June 6, 2012. Miss that one, too, and it will take a breakthrough in medical science for them to have another such opportunity. The next pair of transits will not occur until 2117 and 2125.

The astronomer Johannes Kepler was the first person to recognize the potential for such displays when he wrote in 1627 that Venus would appear against the backdrop of the Sun late in the year 1631. He also realized that meticulous observers at different spots on Earth could use the transit indirectly to calculate the distance to the Sun. An observer in London, say, would see Venus from a different angle than would somebody in Cape Town, South Africa. Knowing the distance between the two cities astronomers could use the angle between the observers to calculate the distance to Venus, and from that, the distance between Earth and the Sun. Kepler died the year

14

before the transit, but he would have missed it anyway, because it happened during the night in Europe and it was visible only on the other side of the Earth.

Although Kepler made tremendous leaps in understanding the motions of the planets, he was not immune to mistakes. He predicted the next transit for the middle of the 18th century, not recognizing that another would occur only eight years later. That 1639 transit would have passed unnoticed by all had it not been for Jeremiah Horrocks, an insightful young man whose accomplishments might have rivaled Isaac Newton's if his life had not ended so early.

Despite the important role he played in astronomy, Horrocks is a historical black hole. Scholars have no records detailing when he was born, what kind of occupation he held, or even what caused his death at the age of 22 or 23.

Born near Lancashire, Horrocks entered the University of Cambridge at age 13 as a sizar—a member of one of the original work-study programs. In return for his tuition, he acted as a servant to a senior fellow. At Cambridge he took an interest in astronomy and started to read the classics in the field, while at the same time perfecting his techniques for observing the sky.

Later a friend named William Crabtree suggested that Horrocks read the work of Kepler, whose ideas were not well received in England at the time. Horrocks recalculated some of Kepler's tables and realized in 1639 that Venus would transit the Sun in just a few weeks' time. By letter, he urged Crabtree to try to observe it as well.

Horrocks set up a telescope in a darkened room and projected the image of the Sun onto a screen. (Looking at the Sun directly, with or without a telescope, can quickly cause blindness.) Not sure of his own calculations, he started watching two days before he anticipated the event, according to Wilbur Applebaum, a Horrocks scholar and an emeritus professor of history at the Illinois Institute of Technology.

On the fateful Sunday, Horrocks was called away on some unknown but urgent business, but returned in time to see the spot of Venus against the Sun's disk just before sunset. Using the limited transit data he collected, he succeeded in measuring the apparent size of Venus.

Horrocks spent the next year perfecting his calculations and writing several drafts of his work. In December 1640, he sent a letter to Crabtree, telling him that the manuscript was almost complete. The two men, who had never met in person, arranged to get together in January. But the day before their scheduled meeting, Horrocks died.

His work on the transit of Venus did not appear until 1662, but Isaac Newton and Robert Hooke learned about the work before its publication. Mr. Applebaum suggests that Horrocks's ideas, in fact, formed the basis for Newton's theory about the motion of the Moon. Newton acknowledged his predecessor by thanking "our countryman Horrox" in his *Principia*.

Immortal Fame

From that quiet beginning in the 17th century, the study of transits turned into a frenzy the next time an opportunity arrived, thanks to the work of Edmond Halley, whose name graces the famed comet. Halley, who was Britain's Astronomer Royal, conceived of a much simpler way to use the transits of Venus to determine planetary distances.

Instead of using angles, Halley suggested that observers in different locales time the duration of the transit. An observer in Europe would see Venus pass across a different part of the Sun than would an observer in Asia; hence the transit would last longer in one spot than another. By determining the time to the nearest second, they could determine how far away Venus was from Earth, says J. Donald Fernie, an emeritus professor of astronomy at the University of Toronto.

Halley knew that he would not live to see the next transit—he died in 1742—and he pleaded with "those curious astronomers who (when I am dead) will have an opportunity of observing these things." He promised "immortal fame and glory" to astronomers whose observations succeeded in improving the measure of the planet's orbits.

His successors took those words to heart. Despite the hazards of 18th-century travel and the various wars raging among European powers, more than 270 teams went off around the world to record the pair of transits later in that century.

The Royal Society of London sent Charles Mason and Jeremiah Dixon to Sumatra to witness the 1761 event. Only hours into their trip, their ship came under fire from a French frigate in the English Channel. With 11 dead and dozens injured, the British ship returned to port. The rattled scientists sent word to the Royal Society thanking it for the opportunity but graciously declining a second attempt. The society bullied Mason and Dixon into setting off again, however, by threatening their careers and their social standing. Now pressed for time, the two never made it to Sumatra but stopped in South Africa and successfully observed the transit from there.

Mason and Dixon's trials pale in comparison with the sufferings of French astronomers of the time, whose exploits have become legendary in the annals of science. One of them, Guillaume Joseph Hyacinthe Jean Baptiste Le Gentil de la Galaisiere embarked on an ill-fated journey that stretched almost as long as his name.

Le Gentil, as he has come to be known, planned to observe the June 6, 1761 transit from Pondicherry, a French-controlled city on the east coast of India. He left France in March 1760 and arrived at the island of Mauritius, in the southern Indian Ocean, that July. Although he had plenty of time to reach Pondicherry, ill winds and British forces conspired to keep him away. Had he stayed put on Mauritius, he could have observed the transit there. But by bad luck, Le Gentil was at sea trying to reach Pondicherry during the transit and could make no meaningful observations.

Determined not to miss the next one, he decided to remain in the Indian Ocean for several years, studying Madagascar and nearby islands. In 1766 he sailed to Manila to prepare for observing the 1769 transit from there. He tried to circumvent any political problems by requesting letters of recommendation from the Spanish royal court to give to the Spanish governor of Manila. After 14 months the letters arrived, but the governor declared that they must be forgeries because he could not conceive of a response from Europe arriving so quickly.

Le Gentil worried that he might land in prison or suffer a worse fate if he stayed in Manila, so he decided to head back to India. In March 1768, he finally reached Pondicherry, built an observatory, and prepared for the morning of June 4, 1769, when all his years of effort would reach a climax.

The whole month of May brought beautiful weather, and the night of June 3 was clear enough for the astronomer to see a moon of Jupiter. But at 2 a.m., when he awoke to check the conditions, "I saw with the greatest astonishment that the sky was covered every-where . . . From that moment on, I felt doomed I threw myself on my bed, without being able to close my eyes," he said in his published account, translated by the late Helen Sawyer Hogg.

The blanket of clouds blocked out the Sun until after the transit ended—and then the sky cleared for the rest of the day. Le Gentil had missed his last chance, while conditions in Manila that day had remained per-fectly clear.

"That is the fate which often awaits astrono-mers," he wrote. "I had gone more than ten thousand leagues; it seemed that I had crossed such a great expanse of seas, exiling myself from my native lands, only to be the spectator of a fatal cloud which came to place itself before the Sun at the precise moment of my observation, to carry off from me the fruits of my pains and my fatigues."

Le Gentil's luck turned no better when he tried to head home. He made several attempts, only to be blocked by a hurricane on one voyage and by a petulant French captain, who refused him passage, on another.

When the wayward astronomer finally returned to France, after an absence of 11 years, he found his estate in a shambles and his spot occupied in the Academy of Sciences—an outrage considering that the academy had sent him on his trip in the first place. He eventually regained his position, married, had a daughter, and lived until the age of 67.

Difficult Measures

However long and trying, Le Gentil's odyssey was a vacation in contrast to the fate of his colleague Jean-Baptiste Chappe D'Auteroche, who in 1760 slogged overland to the Ural Mountains to observe the transit from there. After that mission proved a success, Chappe requested a warmer climate for the next transit, and the Academy of Sciences sent him to Baja California for the 1769 event. His crew sailed to the east coast of Mexico and crossed the country overland, fighting heat, rain, insects, and rough terrain.

Chappe's engineer, a man known to history only as Pauly, wrote that "high mountains, dreadful precipices, dry deserts offered to us every day some new dangers.

We came near dying a thousand times." They finally reached the Pacific and went by boat to the southern tip of Baja. When they arrived, though, Pauly said, "some savage people who came to us informed us that a most dreadful epidemic was laying waste the county."

With only 13 days left before the 1769 transit, Chappe waved off the warning to move north. Instead his team quickly built an observatory and observed the transit. Days later, the disease starting claiming the Europeans. "A burning soil such as there is in that country was our bed," wrote Pauly. "The few medicines we had brought from France were useless for want of knowing how to use them. In that miserable situation we were bound, to quench our burning thirst, to drink stagnant water full of copper."

Chappe died on August 1, and most of the rest of the team also perished. Pauly survived and carried the observations back to the Academy of Sciences.

Astronomers back in Paris reaped the benefits of such extravagant and ill-fated efforts. Using the hard-won data from Chappe and others, the scientists calculated the astronomical unit to be a little more than 90 million miles, close to the actual value of nearly 93 million miles. But the 18th-century observers had run into an unforeseen difficulty in timing the transits. Nobody, it seemed, could agree on how to tell when Venus began intersecting the disk of the Sun.

The problem was that the planet did not cleanly meet up with the edge of the sun. Instead, as the two bodies neared, the black circle of Venus would seem to ooze toward the edge of the Sun, like oil spreading across a table. That made it difficult for two observers, even right next to each other, to agree on when Venus actually entered and exited the solar disk.

Captain Cook, observing the 1769 transit from Tahiti, described the problem in his journal. Despite perfectly clear skies, "we very distinctly saw an Atmosphere or dusky shade round the body of the Planet which very much disturbed the times of the Contacts," he wrote, ". . . and we differed from one another in Observing the times of the Contacts much more than could be expected."

Scientists once attributed the problem, called the black-drop effect, to the atmosphere of Venus. But new research points toward the Sun itself, and the way it grows darker toward its edges, which can cause strange optical tricks.

The Patriotism Card

More than a century after Cook's voyage, the United States banked on the new technique of photography to get around the dreaded black-drop effect. To secure the necessary support, the superintendent of the U.S. Naval Observatory played the patriotism card by saying that observing the 1874 transit would "afford our countrymen a peculiarly favorable opportunity to exercise their inventive ingenuity in the introduction of improved modes of observation." He helped his case by noting that Britain, Russia, and Germany had provided significant money for their astronomers, says Mr. Dick, the NASA historian.

Congress appropriated a total of $177,000 (the equivalent of more than $2-million today) to send teams of observers to Vladivostok, Russia; Nagasaki, Japan; Beijing; the Kerguelen Islands, in the Indian Ocean; two places in Tasmania; New Zealand; and the Chatham Islands, near New Zealand.

In 1882 Congress appropriated $85,000 to finance another eight expeditions, several of which could stay closer to home because the transit was visible from the United States. Virtually every telescope in the country, says Mr. Dick, was turned toward the Sun on December 6 to witness the transit.

For John Philip Sousa, the 1882 event provided inspiration for a "Transit of Venus March," which was performed early the next year, according to an exhibit titled "Chasing Venus: Observing the Transits of Venus. 1631-2004," on display at the Smithsonian Institution's National Museum of American History through April 2005. Even decades later, the planetary encounter continued to move Sousa, who wrote a comic novel in 1920 called *The Transit of Venus*, about a group of men taking a holiday away from women to watch the transit.

For scientists, though, the transit work was serious business. William Harkness, a Naval Observatory astronomer, used the data collected by the observing teams to calculate a value of 92,797,000 miles, plus or minus 59,700 miles, for the distance between the Earth and Sun. His finding represented a significant improvement over the past century's work, coming within 0.17 percent of the actual value. But astronomers had hoped for even better results. Just a year after Harkness made his calculation, his colleague Simon Newcomb used measurements of the speed of light to calculate the astronomical unit with more than twice the accuracy of Harkness's work. That technique and others eventually eclipsed the transit method for measuring the size of the solar system.

So when Venus appears in front of the Sun next month, astronomers will use the event for other purposes. Mr. Pasachoff, of Williams College, will travel to Greece to study the black-drop effect and to collect data on Venus's atmosphere. He and others will also take advantage of the transit to refine their techniques for studying so-called exoplanets around far-off stars.

Astronomers in the past decade have found more than 100 exoplanets, but it is difficult to measure their sizes and to determine whether they have atmospheres. By watching how the Sun's light changes when Venus transits, researchers can learn how to study transits of exoplanets passing in front of their own parent stars.

While astronomy professors test out new techniques on June 8, high-school students around the world will be recreating history, trying to repeat the work of Harkness and his predecessors who measured the astronomical unit. "We're very excited about this opportunity to bring an exceedingly rare astronomical event before millions of students," says Mr. Pasachoff, who is president of an education panel of the International Astronomical Union. He hopes that the transit will spark students' interest in science and inspire the next generation of astronomy professors.

More than a century ago, Harkness also recognized the power of Venus's appearance before the Sun. He viewed the event as the chance of a lifetime—one that marked major milestones in scientific achievement whenever it came.

With an eye toward history, he wrote in defense of his efforts that "when the last transit season occurred the intellectual world was awakening from the slumber of ages, and that wondrous scientific activity which has led to our present advanced knowledge was just beginning."

Another opportunity would not come until "the June flowers are blooming in 2004," he wrote. "What will be the state of science when the next transit season arrives God only knows. Not even our children's children will live to take part in the astronomy of that day. As for ourselves, we have to do with the present."

Sky watchers as far back as the ancient Greeks have attempted to determine the size of our solar system. Once the distance between Earth and the Sun (the astronomical unit, or AU) had been determined, it was then used as a measurement to describe the distance between the Sun and the other planets and objects in our solar system. The following article, found in Astronomy, *describes how scientists at the Universities of Michigan and Arizona are trying*

to determine the distance from the Sun to the outer edge of the solar system. This distance is estimated to be 55 AU, or fifty-five times the distance between Earth and the Sun. They arrived at this number by detecting Kuiper Belt objects, which are remnants of the original material that formed the planets. —HH

"Edge of the Solar System"
by Richard Talcott
Astronomy, **March 2001**

When ancient mariners set sail into the ocean, their crews no doubt wondered if they might fall off the edge of the world. Astronomers today are more intrigued by real edges, even if they remain elusive, such as where our solar system comes to an end. Now three researchers think they've found the edge, and it's just a stone's throw beyond Pluto.

Lynne Allen and Gary Bernstein of the University of Michigan and Renu Malhotra of the University of Arizona's Lunar and Planetary Laboratory set out to find the edge by looking for distant Kuiper Belt Objects. More than 300 of these objects, remnants of the process that formed the planets some 4.5 billion years ago, have been found in the past 10 years.

Yet none of these lies more than about 55 astronomical units from the sun. (One AU is the average distance from the sun to Earth, or about 93 million miles.) That compares with Neptune's distance of 30 AU and Pluto, which ranges between 30 and 50 AU. The question for the planetary scientists was whether the solar system really ends beyond Pluto or whether more distant objects were simply too faint to be seen.

Keep in mind that the researchers were only interested in where objects formed. So they didn't consider the limit of the sun's gravitational or magnetic influence or the countless comets that orbit far beyond Pluto. Planetary scientists think those comets all formed inside Pluto's orbit and were later ejected.

The team decided to search six areas of sky, each about the size of the full moon, with a state-of-the-art electronic camera. The camera was sensitive enough to pick up any Kuiper Belt Object at least 100 miles in diameter out to 65 AU. They discovered 24 new objects, 9 of them 100 miles across or bigger, but the farthest again lay near the outer part of Pluto's orbit.

The observations provide the best evidence yet that the apparent edge of the solar system is also a real one. But the researchers don't know whether the primordial solar system was simply small, a passing star stripped away more distant objects, or some other process banished the objects. The debate likely won't be settled as easily as by sailing around the world.

Distances within our solar system are measured using astronomical units. For almost everything else, such as the distance to stars and galaxies,

the unit is the parsec. Though astronomers use many different units, the parsec is the most common. A parsec is defined as the distance from which Earth and Sun would appear to be separated from one another by one arc second. An arc second is an angular size, 1/3600 of a degree. That is about the width of the period at the end of this sentence as seen from 100 yards away. One parsec is equal to 1.9 x 10^{13} miles (3.1 x 10^{13} km) or 206,265 AU. The nearest star is about 1.3 parsecs from Earth. The farthest known galaxy is several billion parsecs away.

A more familiar unit of distance in astronomy is the light-year, defined as the distance that light travels in a year. Astronomers often use light-years when they are speaking to the general public. Otherwise, they almost exclusively use the parsec. In the following article from Sky and Telescope, author Ken Croswell explains why he believes the light-year to be a superior unit despite its lack of acceptance in professional astronomy. —HH

"Light-Years Ahead"
by Ken Croswell
Sky and Telescope, April 1995

Some time ago I showed a popular-level science article of mine to a professional astronomer. He glanced at it and chuckled. "Light-years, huh?" It seems I had committed a cardinal sin: I gave distances to stars in light-years, which for some reason are frowned upon in professional astronomy. Professionals prefer the parsec (equal to 3.26 light-years), and when they don't use parsecs they use kiloparsecs or megaparsecs. This preference is so pervasive that hardly any scientific paper dares to mention the humble light-year.

I don't understand the disdain with which professionals regard the light-year, for in almost every way it is the superior unit. Unlike the parsec, the light-year is tied to a fundamental physical constant—the speed of light—which is arguably the most important of all physical constants. It is especially vital to astronomers, whose observations of the cosmos depend on gathering light of one wavelength or another. In addition, the speed of light is the ultimate speed limit in the universe. It appears in Einstein's equation $E = mc^2$ which governs how stars convert their mass into the energy that eventually emerges as the light astronomers see. By contrast, the parsec is a function of the Earth-Sun distance and of the definition of an arc second. Neither quantity is something that observers throughout the universe would know.

Moreover, the light-year, unlike the parsec, conveys to ordinary people the vast scale of astronomical distances. Since light is fast, anyone can deduce that the distance light travels in a year is enormous. Compare this with the parsec, which to most people means nothing. A parsec is the distance of a star whose annual parallax as seen from Earth is 1 arc second, and few people know the definition of parallax or the size of an arc second.

The light-year is likewise much easier to understand. Even those who don't know the definition can usually figure it out. I once showed a three-dimensional map of the nearest stars to someone and told him that the farthest stars on the map were 12 light-years from the Sun. He wasn't familiar with the term, but he said, "A light-year—let me see—that must be the distance that light travels in one year, right?" If I had told him the distance in parsecs, he would have given me a blank stare.

The light-year offers another advantage, by immediately revealing how long a star's light takes to reach Earth. If you know that Arcturus is 34 light-years away, you also know that the gleam you see from Arcturus left there 34 years ago. What could be simpler?

In addition to being natural and intuitive the light-year relates to three other units of measurement: the inch, the mile, and the distance between the Earth and the Sun. It turns out that the number of Earth-Sun distances in a light-year (63,240) almost exactly equals the number of inches in a mile (63,360). This, too, conveys to people the great size of astronomical distances, but this time it does so quantitatively.

By contrast, the parsec has little to recommend it, except that most professional astronomers currently use it. Its only advantage is its relation to a star's parallax, since inverting the parallax gives the star's distance in parsecs. For example, a star with a parallax of 0.1 arc second is 10 parsecs away, and a star with a parallax of

0.01 arc second is 100 parsecs away. But this advantage is minor because few astronomers measure parallaxes, and those who do can easily multiply their result by 3.26 to put the result into light-years. Furthermore, most stars and all galaxies are so distant that their parallaxes are too tiny to measure, so what is the point of using a unit that is based on these objects' supposed parallaxes?

Ah, but here it would seem we go against long-standing tradition. After all, everyone knows that astronomers have always used parsecs, whereas light-years are a modern invention. Well, "everyone" is wrong. Contrary to the belief of most professionals, light-years are the traditional unit they were used before anyone dreamed up the parsec.

To argue from tradition one can do no better than go back to 1838, when Prussian astronomer Friedrich Wilhelm Bessel first determined the parallax of a star other than the Sun. Bessel's discovery was a major breakthrough, as astronomers since Copernicus had looked for but failed to find stellar parallax. Some geocentrically inclined people even used this failure to argue that the Earth did not orbit the Sun,

Bessel's lucky star was 61 Cygni, which he began studying more than a quarter century earlier, Although 61 Cygni is faint, Bessel took notice of its large proper motion, a sign that the star was nearby and so had a measurable parallax. When Bessel succeeded in determining the star's parallax, he gave the distance in light-years, not parsecs. As he wrote in *Monthly Notices of the Royal Astronomical Society*, "We find the distance of the star 61 Cygni from the sun 657,700 mean distances of the earth from the sun: light employs 10.3 years to traverse this distance."

In contrast, parsecs—like car alarms and drive-by shootings—are an unfortunate creation of the 20th century. Indeed, when this awkward unit first entered astronomy, astronomers themselves debated both its merits and what to call it. A 1913 article by Lick Observatory astronomer Heber Curtis—who later argued that spiral nebulae were other galaxies outside our own—noted that the parsec was variously called the macron, the astron, and the astrometer as well.

In his article Curtis came out strongly in favor of the light-year, calling it the unit that reveals the enormous distances of space and makes sense to the layperson. "So completely does the customary and well-known unit of the light-year fill all these requirements," he wrote, "that any change appears to me not only to be entirely unnecessary, but even to savor a little of pedantry."

The points Curtis made then are even more valid today, when astronomy is further removed from the average person. Not only does the light-year conveniently express the distances of stars and galaxies, but it also helps bridge the vast distance between professional astronomers and the public. It is, in short, light-years ahead of any competing unit.

Ken Croswell, "Light-Years Ahead," *Sky and Telescope*, April 1995. Copyright © 1995 by Sky Publishing Corp. Reproduced with permission of the publisher.

Astronomers have long pondered the size of the universe. The following article from CNN.com reports an estimate of the universe's size in light-years. One light-year is the distance that light travels in one year. The speed of light is 186,000 miles per second (300,000 kilometers per second). So, in one year, light travels almost 6 trillion miles (10 trillion km). This article describes how a group of researchers, including Neil Cornish of Montana State University, reached their conclusion about the universe's size after examining primordial radiation that had been imprinted on the cosmos. This measurement takes into account the fact that the universe has been expanding since its beginning 13.7 billion years ago. Cornish's group also tackled the question of whether the universe was finite or infinite, but the results were inconclusive. —HH

"Universe 156 Billion Light-Years Wide"
by Robert Roy Britt
Space.com, May 24, 2004

The universe is at least 156 billion light-years wide.

In the new study, researchers examined primordial radiation imprinted on the cosmos. Among their conclusions is that it is less likely that there is some crazy cosmic "hall of mirrors" that would cause one object to be visible in two locations. And they've ruled out the idea that we could peer deep into space and time and see our own planet in its youth.

Stretching Reality

The universe is about 13.7 billion years old. Light reaching us from the earliest known galaxies has been traveling, therefore, for more than 13 billion years. So one might assume that the radius of the universe is 13.7 billion light-years and that the whole shebang is double that, or 27.4 billion light-years wide.

But the universe has been expanding ever since the beginning of time, when theorists believe it all sprang forth from an infinitely dense point in a Big Bang.

"All the distance covered by the light in the early universe gets increased by the expansion of the universe," explains Neil Cornish, an astrophysicist at Montana State University. "Think of it like compound interest."

Need a visual? Imagine the universe just a million years after it was born, Cornish suggests. A batch of light travels for a year, covering one light-year. "At that time, the universe was about 1,000 times smaller than it is today," he said. "Thus, that one light-year has now stretched to become 1,000 light-years."

All the pieces add up to 78 billion light-years. The light has not traveled that far, but "the starting point of a photon reaching us today after traveling for 13.7 billion years is now 78 billion light-years away," Cornish said. That would be the radius of the universe, and twice that—156 billion light-years—is the diameter. That's based on a view going 90 percent of the way back in time, so it might be slightly larger.

"It can be thought of as a spherical diameter is the usual sense," Cornish added comfortingly.

(You might have heard the universe is almost surely flat, not spherical. The flatness refers to its geometry being "normal," like what is taught in school; two parallel lines can never cross.)

Hall of Mirrors

The scientists studied the cosmic microwave background, radiation unleashed about 380,000 years after the Big Bang, when the universe had first expanded enough to cool and allow atoms to form. Temperature differences in the background radiation left an imprint on the sky that was used last year to reveal the age of the universe and confirm other important cosmological measurements.

The cosmic background radiation is like a baby picture of the cosmos, before any stars were born.

The focus of the new work, which was published last week in the journal *Physical Review Letters*, was a search of background radiation data for paired circles that would have indicated the universe is like a hall of mirrors, in which multiple images of the same object could show up in different locations in space-time. A hall of mirrors could mean the universe is finite but tricks us into thinking it is infinite.

Think of it as a video game in which an object disappearing on the right side of the screen reappears on the left.

"Several years ago we showed that any finite universe in which light had time to 'wrap around' since the Big Bang would have the same pattern of cosmic microwave background temperature fluctuations around pairs of circles," Cornish explained. They looked for the most likely patterns that would be evident to NASA's Wilkinson Microwave Anisotropy Probe.

They didn't find those patterns.

Don't Look Back

"Our results don't rule out a hall-of-mirrors effect, but they make the possibility far less likely," Cornish said, adding that the findings have shown "no sign that the universe is finite, but that doesn't prove that it is infinite."

The results do render impossible a "soccer ball" shape for the universe, proposed late last year by another team. "However, if they were to 'pump up' their soccer ball to make it larger, they could evade our bounds" and still be in the realm of possibility, Cornish said. Other complex shapes haven't been ruled out.

The findings eliminate any chance of seeing our ancient selves, however, unless we can master time travel.

"If the universe was finite, and had a size of about 4 billion to 5 billion light-years, then light would be able to wrap around the universe, and with a big enough telescope we could view the Earth just after it solidified and when the first life formed," Cornish said. "Unfortunately, our results rule out this tantalizing possibility."

One way to theorize about the universe is through the use of mathematical models. Mathematical models use mathematical language to describe the behavior of a system. Since ancient times, many have attempted to explain the motions they observed in the heavens with geometrical models. As science progressed over the years, these models were changed to fit current observations and theories. The following article from National Forum *shows the evolution of the model of planetary motion, ultimately ending with Kepler's three laws of planetary motion. Kepler's laws state that (1) each planet moves around the Sun in an elliptical orbit with the Sun at one focus of the ellipse, (2) the imaginary line joining each planet to the Sun (called the radius vector) sweeps through equal areas of space in equal amounts of time as the planet moves along the orbital path, and (3) the square of a planet's orbital period around *the Sun is directly proportional to the cube of the planet's mean distance from the Sun. —HH*

"The Failure of Theory: Models of the Solar System"
by Daniel Berger
National Forum, **Winter 2001**

It is commonly believed that science operates entirely by the test of observation; theories explain observations, but observations are trumps and can override any theory—even when no new theory is available to explain the observations. This is a myth, since most observations require a theoretical framework or conceptual model to make sense, and some observations can be explained by more than one theory or model. For this reason, scientists are reluctant to accept models—or even observations—that fly in the face of an accepted theory, especially if that theory is well supported.

In ancient times, it was obvious that the Moon went around the earth. This was obvious because it is true.

The ancients also noticed the Sun moving around the earth—a perfectly reasonable explanation of its apparent motion, and the simplest one available. When other moving heavenly bodies—as distinct from the "fixed stars"—were discovered, it seemed obvious that they, too, went around the earth; this is the geocentric model of the universe. The ancients had deduced the correct shape of the earth by about

39

700–600 b.c., and the size of the earth was correctly estimated by Eratosthenes of Alexandria in about 500 b.c.

There was a physical theory to explain both the geocentric model and the spherical Earth. By 500 b.c. or so,
the most widely accepted scientific ideas held that the
world below the Moon was made of four elements
(earth, air, water, fire), which "gravitated" toward the
center. It was pretty obvious that if you let go of anything except air or fire, it fell. Furthermore, fire rose
through air, so air must naturally tend to be lower than
fire. This meant that the earth was made of, in ascend-
ing order, a sphere of earth, a sphere of water, a
sphere of air, and a sphere of fire—which was blamed
for the "char marks" on the moon. On the other hand,
the heavenly bodies did not fall. Therefore, they must
be made of something different (the fifth element or
"quintessence"). Because the heavenly bodies were
observed to move around the earth, this fifth element
must have the property of moving in circles.

In the second century a.d., Claudius Ptolemy
organized astronomical and physical knowledge into
what is now known as the Ptolemaic system. The earth
was at the center, because that is what both observation and theory indicated. Heliocentric (sun-centered)
models had been proposed for religious reasons (Sun
= God), but they were not supported by the evidence
or by theory. Ptolemy's model stood the test of naked-
eye observation for many centuries.

By the sixteenth century a.d., naked-eye observations had improved, and problems were becoming
apparent in the geocentric system. Because everybody

assumed that heavenly bodies moved in perfect circles, observational discrepancies were explained by adding epicycles, or circles on circles. Some versions of the Ptolemaic system had three or four levels of epicycles, and Nicolaus Copernicus (1473–1543) realized that a heliocentric system could eliminate one or two, but not all, levels of epicycles.

Thus, a heliocentric universe was inferred from the facts that the geocentric system was becoming unwieldy and that a heliocentric model provided a simpler explanation. There was no observational evidence to unequivocally prove, or even to indicate, that the earth moved around the Sun! And the best physical theory of the time denied that a moving Earth was possible: the earth, being made of gross matter, should fall to the "bottom of the universe," the center.

The discovery by Galileo Galilei (1564–1642) of the four large moons of Jupiter showed that it was perfectly possible for heavenly bodies to circle other heavenly bodies. For Galileo, this supported the Copernican model. But Galileo was one of the few; for many astronomers, the observation was irrelevant, if not an artifact of Galileo's telescope. More heavenly bodies moving in circles: ho-hum.

The heliocentric model was hotly disputed by the best astronomer of the sixteenth century, Tycho Brahe (1546–1601). While Tycho acknowledged that Copernicus had succeeded in removing a few epicycles, he proposed a system that kept Copernicus' best results while avoiding the serious difficulty of finding an explanation for a moving Earth. In Tycho's system the

Sun moves around the earth, dragging the rest of the planets with it. This is exactly equivalent, on the basis of ground-based observation, to a heliocentric model.

Without invoking supernatural help, it was impossible to explain why a moving Earth would not fall to the center of a heliocentric universe. And if the planets (including the Sun) were made of something else—the quintessence—why couldn't they naturally move in circles, just as earthly matter naturally fell to the center?

But were the heavenly bodies really made of a fifth element? Galileo's other telescopic discoveries—mountains on the Moon, spots on the Sun, irregular and blemish-like surface features on Mars—implied that the heavens were made of the same substances as the earth. If the heavenly bodies were made of earth, why didn't they fall to the center? Astronomy was at an impasse: what naturalistic model could explain the heavens? The heavenly bodies moved: how could they do so without constant and blatant divine intervention?

Tycho's top pupil, Johannes Kepler (1571–1630), inherited his master's observations: the best naked-eye astronomy ever performed. Kepler was convinced of the heliocentric system for religious reasons, and set himself the task of proving it from Tycho's immense fund of data.

Kepler clung stubbornly to the heliocentric theory, while painfully discarding model after model until he had one that fit the best observations of his day exactly. When the dust cleared, he not only did not need epicycles, but he also had reduced the perfect circles of astronomical theory to ellipses. Kepler's Laws of

Planetary Motion were not supported by any scientific explanation or theory. They were empirical; Kepler was reduced to the speculation that the planets were moved in their orbits by angels.

Once it was convincingly shown that Kepler's model fit observations better than any geocentric model, the system of five elements and perfect circles began to collapse. Astronomy became a field without a theory, and physics and chemistry were alike bereft of their guiding principle. Kepler's Laws remained purely empirical for almost a century until Isaac Newton (1642–1727) was able to explain them by his Theory of Universal Gravitation.

Isaac Newton developed a broad and far-reaching theory of gravitation that would apply not only to apples falling from trees but also to the motion of the planets orbiting the Sun. This was called the universal law of gravitation. This mathematical model shows that the force of gravity between two objects is inversely proportional to the square of the distance between them. Newton came to this conclusion after studying Kepler's first law of planetary motion, which states that each planet moves around the Sun in an elliptical orbit with the Sun at one

focus of the ellipse. It is "universal" because all objects in the universe are attracted to each other according to this relationship. In the following article from Natural History, *Neil de Grasse Tyson, an astrophysicist and director of the Hayden Planetarium in New York City, discusses how the universality of the physical laws, such as gravity, helps us to understand the workings of the universe.* —HH

"On Earth as in the Heavens"
by Neil de Grasse Tyson
Natural History, **November 2000**

Until Isaac Newton wrote down the universal law of gravitation, there was little reason to presume that the laws of physics on Earth were the same as elsewhere in the universe. Earth had earthly things going on, and the heavens had heavenly things going on. Indeed according to many scholars of the day, the heavens were unknowable to our feeble mortal minds. When Newton breached this philosophical barrier by rendering motion comprehensible and predictable some theologians criticized him for leaving nothing for the Creator to do. Newton had figured out that the force of gravity pulling ripe apples from branches also guides tossed objects along their curved trajectories and directs the Moon in its orbit around Earth.

The universality of physical laws drives scientific discovery like nothing else. Gravity was just the beginning. Imagine the excitement among nineteenth-century astronomers when laboratory prisms, which break light beams into the colors of the spectrum, were first turned to the Sun. Spectra are not only beautiful but contain oodles of information about the light emitting object including its temperature and composition. Chemical elements are revealed as unique patterns of light or dark bands that cut across the spectrum. To people's delight and amazement, the chemical signatures in the light emitted by the Sun were identical to those identified in the laboratory. No longer the exclusive tool of chemists, the prism showed that the Sun, as different as it is from Earth in size, mass, temperature, and appearance, contains the same stuff—hydrogen, carbon, oxygen, nitrogen, calcium, iron, and so forth. But more important than our laundry list of shared ingredients was the recognition that the laws of physics prescribing the formation of these spectral signatures on Earth are also operating on the Sun, 93 million miles away.

So fertile was this concept of universality that it was successfully applied in reverse. Further analysis of the Sun's spectrum revealed the signature of an element that had no known counterpart on Earth. The new substance was given a name derived from the Greek word for Sun (*helios*) and was only later observed in the lab. Thus helium became the first—and only—element in the chemist's periodic table to be discovered someplace other than on Earth.

OK, the laws of physics work in our solar system, but do they work across the galaxy? Across the universe? Across time itself? Step by step, the laws were tested. As with geologists reading Earth's history in stratified sediments, the farther away we look in space, the farther back we see in time. Spectra from the universe's most distant objects, whose light has been traveling for billions of years, show the same chemical signatures we see everywhere else. Indeed, a mathematical quantity known as the fine-structure constant, which controls the basic fingerprinting for every element, must have remained unchanged for billions of years.

Of course, not all objects and phenomena in the cosmos have versions of themselves on Earth. You've probably never walked through a cloud of glowing million-degree plasma, and you've probably never greeted a black hole on the street. What matters is the universality of the laws of physics that describe these phenomena. When spectral analyses were first applied to the light emitted by interstellar nebulae, a signature was discovered that had no counterpart on Earth. At that time, the periodic table of elements had few empty boxes (when helium was discovered, there were two dozen). Astrophysicists invented the name nebulium to serve as a placeholder until they could figure out exactly what was going on. It turned out that in space, gaseous nebulae are so rarefied that atoms go long stretches without colliding with one another. Under these conditions, electrons within atoms behaved in ways that had never before been seen in labs on Earth. The hypothetical nebulium was simply the signature of ordinary oxygen doing extraordinary things.

The universality of physical laws tells us that if we land on another planet with a thriving alien civilization, it will be running on the same laws that we have discovered and tested here on Earth—even if the aliens harbor different social and political beliefs. Furthermore, if you want to talk to the aliens, you can bet they won't speak English or French or even Mandarin. Nor will you know whether shaking their hands—if indeed they have hands to shake—would be considered an act of war or of peace. Your best hope will be to find a way to communicate in the language of science.

Such an attempt was made with the *Pioneer 10* and *11* and *Voyager 1* and *2* spacecraft, the only ones with enough speed to escape the solar system's gravitational pull. All four spacecraft bore a golden plaque etched with scientific pictograms showing, among other things, the Sun's location in the Milky Way galaxy and the structure of the hydrogen atom. *Voyager* also carried recorded sounds from Mother Earth, including the sound of a human heartbeat, whale songs, and selections of music ranging from Beethoven to Chuck Berry. While these offerings humanized the message, it's not clear whether they would mean a thing to alien ears— assuming aliens have ears in the first place. My favorite parody of this gesture was a *Saturday Night Live* skit that appeared shortly after the *Voyager* launch. The aliens who recovered the spacecraft had only one reply for Earthlings: "Send more Chuck Berry."

Science thrives not only on the universality of physical laws but also on the existence and persistence of physical constants. As already noted, the fine structure constant controls the spectral patterns made by elements. The constant of gravitation, known to scientists as big G, enables Newton's equation to calculate the exact strength of gravitational force. Big G has been implicitly tested for variation over eons. If you do the math, you can determine that a star's luminosity is steeply dependent on it. In other words, if big G had been even slightly different in the past, the energy output of the Sun would have been far more variable than anything that the biological, climatological, or geological records indicate, In fact, there are no known time-dependent or location—dependent fundamental constants—they all appear to be truly constant.

Of all physical constants, the speed of light is probably the most famous. No matter how powerful your engines, you will never overtake a beam of light. Why not? No experiment ever conducted has revealed any object reaching the speed of light, and well-tested laws of physics predict and account for that. I know these statements sound closed-minded. True, some of the most embarrassing predictions believed to have been made in the name of science have underestimated the ingenuity of engineers: "We will never fly." "Flying will never be commercially feasible." "We will never fly faster than the speed of sound." "We will never split the atom." "We will never go to the Moon." You've heard them. But what these predictions have in common is that no established law of physics was invoked to support the claim.

On the other hand, the claim "we will never outrun a beam of light" is a qualitatively different prediction. It flows from time-tested physical principles. Yes, highway signs for interstellar travelers of the future will surely read: THE SPEED OF LIGHT: IT'S

NOT JUST A GOOD IDEA. IT'S THE LAW. The good thing about the laws of physics is that they require no law-enforcement agencies (although I do own a geeky T-shirt that says OBEY GRAVITY).

Another class of universal truths are the conservation laws. Under their jurisdiction, certain measured entities remain unchanged *no matter what*. The three most important of these laws are the conservation of mass and energy, the conservation of linear and angular momentum and the conservation of electric charge. These laws are in evidence everywhere, from the domain of particle physics to the large-scale structure of the universe.

In spite of this boasting, all is not perfect in paradise. It happens that we cannot see, touch, or taste the source of 90 percent of the gravity of the universe. This mysterious dark matter, which remains undetected except for its gravitational pull on matter we do detect, may be composed of exotic particles yet to be identified. A minority of astrophysicists, however, have suggested that there *is* no dark matter—you just need to modify Newton's law of gravity. Simply add a few terms to the equations, and all will be well.

Perhaps one day we'll learn that Newton's gravity indeed requires adjustment. That'll be OK. It happened once before. In 1915 Albert Einstein came up with the general theory of relativity, which reformulated the principles of gravity so that they applied to objects of extremely high mass, a category unknown to Newton and for which his law of gravity breaks down. The lesson here is that our confidence in a law's universality flows from the range of conditions in which it has been tested and verified. The broader this range, the more powerfully that law can describe the cosmos. For ordinary household gravity, Newton's law (still) works just fine. For black holes and the large-scale structure of the universe, however, we need general relativity. Each law works flawlessly in its own domain, wherever that domain may be in the universe.

To the scientist, the universality of physical laws makes the cosmos a marvelously simple place. The psychologist's domain—human nature—is infinitely more complex. In America, classroom curricula can be determined by school board members who vote according to the prevailing social and political winds. Around the world, varying belief systems lead to political differences that are not always resolved peacefully. And some people talk to bus stanchions. The miracle of physical laws is that they apply everywhere, whether or not you choose to believe in them. After the laws of physics, everything else is opinion.

Not that scientists don't argue. We do—a lot. When we do, however, we are usually expressing opinions about the interpretation of ratty data on the frontier of our knowledge. Wherever and whenever a physical law can be invoked in the discussion, the debate is guaranteed to be brief: No, your idea for a perpetual motion machine will never work—it violates laws of thermodynamics. No, you can't build a time machine that will enable you to go back and prevent your parents from ever meeting each other—it violates causality laws. And without violating momentum laws, you cannot spontaneously levitate and hover above the ground, whether or not you are seated in the lotus position (although you could possibly perform this stunt if you managed to let forth a powerful and sustained exhaust of flatulents).

Knowledge of physical laws can, in some cases, give you the confidence to confront surly people. A few years ago, I was having a hot cocoa nightcap at a dessert shop in Pasadena, California. I had ordered it with whipped cream, of course. When it arrived at the table, I saw no trace of the stuff. After I told the waiter my cocoa had no whipped cream, he asserted that I couldn't see it because it had sunk to the bottom. Since whipped cream has a very low density and floats on all liquids that humans consume, I offered the waiter two possible explanations: either somebody forgot to add the whipped cream to my cocoa, or the universal laws of physics were different in his restaurant. Unconvinced, he brought over a dollop of whipped cream to test for himself. After bobbing once or twice in my cup, the whipped cream set up straight, afloat.

What better proof do you need of the universality of physical laws?

Natural History November 2000; copyright © Natural History Magazine, Inc. 2000.

Albert Einstein's special theory of relativity states that the speed of light is the same for all observers, regardless of their motion relative to

*the source of the light. It also states that all
observers who are moving at constant speeds
should observe the same physical laws. Einstein
showed that the only way these ideas were possible was if time intervals and/or lengths change
according to the speed of the system relative to
the observer. In order to determine whether
Einstein's ideas are correct, physicists test
whether the predictions of Einstein's theory
match observations. Many tests have been conducted and Einstein's special theory of relativity
has held true. The following article by Robert
Pool from the journal* Science *describes how
advances in tools such as extremely stable lasers
have made it possible to verify the accuracy of
Einstein's special theory of relativity to greater
and greater degrees.* —HH

"Closing In on Einstein's Special Relativity Theory"
by Robert Pool
Science, November 30, 1990

For a theory that stands as one of the great triumphs of
modern science, Einstein's special theory of relativity
had until recently never stood on a completely firm
experimental footing—the few explicit tests were only
accurate enough to guarantee the formulas of special
relativity to within about 2%. But over the past 11
years, physicists using instruments undreamed of in
Einstein's time have finally fixed that. With such tools

as extremely stable lasers, physicists have now improved the experimental verification of special relativity by a factor of 4,000.

"Of course, in a sense, special relativity had already been well tested because it's at the core of all of modern physics," notes Clifford Will, a physicist at Washington University in St. Louis. Quantum electrodynamics, for instance, includes special relativity in its framework and makes predictions that agree with experiment to a dozen decimal places.

Nevertheless, the verification is comforting—especially for nonphysicists, who sometimes seem to find it difficult to swallow the peculiar predictions of special relativity. The notion that the speed of light does not depend on the motion of the observer, for instance, seems to contradict common sense. Anyone who has ridden a bicycle knows that the relative speed of a head wind increases as you pedal faster into it. And other consequences of Einstein's theory, which says that time and space are relative, are equally strange: A clock that moves at a high speed past an observer will appear to run more slowly, and a fast-moving measuring stick will appear to shrink.

Historically, Einstein was pointed toward his special theory by an experiment performed by Albert Michelson and Edward Morley in 1887. At the time, scientists believed that light traveled in an invisible substance called the ether, which permeated all space; light beams would travel at a fixed velocity in the ether, but they would seem slower or faster to an observer moving with respect to the ether, depending on whether the observer was moving in the same direction as the light or against it.

Michelson and Morley set out to determine how fast the earth was moving through the ether—and got an unexpected result. Their experiment used a system of mirrors to split a light beam into two parts traveling perpendicular to each other and then to recombine the two beams so that they would produce an interference pattern. The researchers reasoned that the earth's motion through the ether should change the observed speeds of the two beams in different ways and influence how they interfered with each other. By rotating their apparatus through 90°, Michelson and Morley expected these velocity shifts to produce a change in the interference pattern that they could use to calculate the earth's speed through the ether.

But the interference patterns didn't change, no matter which way the two scientists turned their apparatus. This implied that the speed of light was the same in every direction—and threw into question the whole concept of the ether.

Eighteen years later, Einstein developed his special theory of relativity, which explained the Michelson-Morley result. But Einstein, depending mostly on his own intuition about how the universe behaved, jumped way ahead of the existing data, and it wasn't until the 1930s that two important confirming experiments were performed.

The Kennedy-Thorndike experiment of 1932 used equipment much like Michelson and Morley's to show that the speed of light in a moving system is independent of the velocity of that system. When linked with its predecessor's conclusion that the speed of light was the same in all directions, this implied that the speed of light is always constant, regardless of its direction or the motion of an observer. In 1938, the Ives-Stillwell experiment measured the frequency of light emitted from fast-moving hydrogen atoms to demonstrate the phenomenon of time dilation—a moving clock seems to go more slowly by a factor of $(1-v^2/c^2)^{-\frac{1}{2}}$, where c is the speed of light and v is the speed of the clock with respect to the observer.

Theoretical physicist H. P. Robertson of Caltech put the finishing touches on the proof in 1949. In a seminal paper, he showed that if certain reasonable assumptions were made about how the universe behaves, then the validity of special relativity could be confirmed from the two 1930s tests plus the Michelson-Morley experiment. However, although all three tests were marvels of experimental technique at the time they were done, their precision was not high by today's standards. The Kennedy-Thorndike experiment, the least accurate, had an uncertainty of 2%. The new age of experimental verification of special relativity did not begin until 1979.

In that year, John Hall and Alain Brillet of the Joint Institute of Laboratory Astrophysics in Boulder, Colorado, performed a modern version of the Michelson-Morley experiment, taking advantage of very stable lasers to get a precision 4,000 times greater than that of the original. "Ours used an optical interference condition like Michelson-Morley," Hall says, but there the similarity ends. Instead of mirrors and primitive light sources, the two physicists used two carefully tuned and very stable lasers. And instead of an interference pattern, they measured the two lasers' "optical heterodyne beat"—a technical characteristic related to the difference between the frequencies of the two lasers.

Despite these differences, the two experiments actually test the same physical phenomenon, Will explains. Both are looking for the presence of a "preferred reference frame" that would serve as a privileged backdrop for the physical workings of nature; in Michelson and Morley's experiment it was the ether, and in Hall and Brillet's it was the cosmic microwave background of the universe. If special relativity were invalid, the outcome of an experiment would be dependent on its motion with respect to that preferred frame.

In their experiment, Hall and Brillet first fixed the frequencies of the two lasers and measured their optical heterodyne beat. They then rotated one of the lasers. As with the Michelson-Morley work, if the lasers moved with respect to some preferred frame, the frequencies of their light should depend on their velocity with respect to that frame. Rotating one laser would then shift that one's frequency but not the other's, thereby altering the beat between them. But Hall and Brillet, like Michelson and Morley, saw no evidence of motion with respect to a fixed reference frame.

Within the past 2 years researchers have also put the other two theoretical underpinnings of special relativity on a precise experimental footing. In 1985, a group of physicists at the University of Aarhus in Denmark and Colorado State University in Fort Collins

used a beam of fast-moving neon atoms for a modern Ives-Stillwell test. When excited by a laser, neon atoms emit light at a precise frequency, so they can be used as clocks; by looking at the variation of the speed of these "clocks" as the Earth moves through space, the researchers measured the time dilation of special relativity to an accuracy of 40 parts per million.

Then in April of this year, Hall and co-worker Dieter Hils put the third leg on the experimental tripod supporting special relativity with an updated Kennedy-Thorndike experiment. "This work allows [special relativity] to be deduced entirely from experiment at an accuracy of 70 parts per million," Hall says—a 300-fold improvement over the previous best. As in the 1979 Hall-Brillet study, the researchers measured the heterodyne beat between two lasers, but with a couple of changes. First, they didn't rotate either laser. Instead, they used two different types, taking advantage of the fact that if special relativity were invalid, the frequencies of the two lasers should change in different ways as their velocities with respect to a preferred reference frame changed. Second, they recorded the heterodyne beat over 24 hours.

As the Earth rotates, the velocity of the lab and the lasers changes with respect to the cosmic ray background. Then if the behavior of the lasers is dependent upon their velocity in this preferred reference frame, the two lasers should be affected differently, causing their heterodyne beat to shift over the 24-hour period. But to a high precision, the researchers saw no change. The experiment would have been impossible, Hall says, without the ability to keep the lasers' frequencies almost perfectly stable over several days—a feat that would have been unachievable only a few years ago.

And it just keeps getting better. "We could probably improve the accuracy [of the 1979 experiment] by a factor of 4,000 now," Hall says. And the Aarhus researchers are expected to announce soon a result with a much more accurate measurement of time dilation. Where will it all stop? "At some point, it's not clear how much you gain [from continuing to test special relativity]," Will says. "I wouldn't necessarily spend millions of dollars to test it further," but as long as experimental advances make it easy to add the extra decimal point, it will probably keep going.

Einstein's theory of general relativity was a result of his effort to remove the restriction on special relativity that no accelerations, and thus no forces, be present. He was then able to apply his ideas to gravitational force. It took Einstein eleven years to formulate his theory of general relativity, and it is our best current theory of gravitation. Einstein's theory of general relativity is used to explain such things as the expansion of the universe and the behavior of black holes and neutron stars. Existing tests had fallen short of proving Einstein's theory of

*general relativity when proposals were made
in the early 1960s to test the theory in space.
The following article from* Science *tells the story
of the Stanford University scientists who were
behind the proposals and their determination
to see the project brought to fruition.* —HH

"Putting Einstein to the Test—In Space"
by Ann Gibbons
Science, November 15, 1991

In the fall of 1959, three scientists were sitting on the
edge of the men's pool on the Stanford University
campus when they came up with a way to test one of
the most influential—but least tested—conceptions in
20th-century science: Einstein's general theory of relativity. One of the three, the internationally known
physicist Leonard Schiff, was just finishing his usual
lunchtime swim when he was introduced by physicist
William Fairbank to a new, young faculty member,
Robert Cannon. Recalls Cannon: "Leonard pulled
himself up on the side of the pool and started talking
about this concept he had about testing Einstein's theory on gravity."

Although Schiff presented his notion as little more
than a "thought experiment," he knew there was one
place where it could be put into practice: space. It was
only 2 years after the launch of Sputnik—and the birth
of the space era—but the trio already had started planning how to use near zero-gravity space as a lab for its
experiment. The idea was elegant: On Earth, the planet's

gravitational field obscures the minuscule gravitational effects predicted by general relativity; but in space, highly sensitive gyroscopes could measure the effect unimpeded—presuming it was there.

Not long after drying off, the three swimmers sketched out an early version of what is now considered one of NASA's most interesting scientific experiments: Gravity Probe B. It took 32 years, the invention of new technologies, countless demonstrations to highly skeptical fellow scientists, and some intense lobbying of Congress, but at last NASA seems about to float Schiff's idea. It was cut from NASA's budget four times, but now the $300-million project is funded at $27.2 million for fiscal year 1992, and a launch is scheduled for 1995 to test the technology on the space shuttle. That is to be followed by a full-fledged satellite mission in 1998. When it finally flies, the scientific payoff for the experiment, under the leadership of Francis Everitt, Bradford Parkinson, and John Turneaure of Stanford (Schiff and Fairbank are no longer alive) could be enormous, because almost all the deepest speculations of modern cosmology—such as those describing the expansion of the universe and the behavior of massive black holes and neutron stars—draw on Einstein's theory of general relativity.

Schiff had been pondering the shortcomings of existing tests of this theory for years, but there was no means to test it in space until the early 1960s, when the newborn NASA began plans for its first Orbiting Astronomical Observatory (OAO). In 1963 the Stanford term made its first pitch to NASA for money—and it hoped to fly its experiment on the OAO. NASA came through with research money but made it clear from the start that it thought the experiment was a long shot, recalls Cannon. "Many of us didn't believe they could do it," says University of Chicago physics professor Eugene Parker, who reviewed the proposal for NASA in the late 1960s. "We thought it was very clever, but we were skeptical that anyone could devise a way to measure such a tiny effect."

Yet over the years the Stanford researchers have leaped over one technological hurdle after another, so that by now their far-fetched idea has gained so much momentum that it will be hard to stop. And most reviewers found the experiment alluring because it takes on aspects of general relativity that previously have been virtually impossible to test directly. Although important progress has been made in the past 30 years to confirm parts of the theory, there are still large holes—and Gravity Probe B's verdict—pro or con— could reverberate throughout all of physics and cosmology. As Irwin Shapiro, director of the Harvard-Smithsonian Center for Astrophysics (CfA), put it in a letter to NASA in 1989: "Gravity Probe B is widely recognized as the most important (fundamental) physics experiment NASA has ever undertaken."

But therein lies an exquisite irony, Gravity Probe B is just the kind of moderately priced, cutting-edge scientific experiment NASA claims it wants to fly in space. And yet because it is an oddball that fails to fit in with the agency's usual astronomy mission goals and because it is competing for scarce resources, NASA administrators have tried to kill the project twice since 1980. But along the way the Stanford researchers have kept the project alive by finding a few key friends inside NASA and Congress, and by acquiring the skills of lobbyists and bureaucratic maneuverers.

It didn't hurt that their experiment offers the romance of testing the ideas of not just one but two great luminaries of physics—Einstein and Newton, whose theories on gravity disagree in important ways. Newton said in his time-honored theory of the universe that gravity is a force transmitted instantaneously over vast distances—a notion challenged by Einstein when he worked out his famous theory of special relativity in 1905, which says that no signal can travel faster than the speed of light. It then follows that gravity could not be a force that travels out from a massive object to tug instantly on everything around it. So Einstein proposed instead in 1916 that gravity is not a force but a "field" that warps space and time (also known as space-time, the continuum in Einstein's four-dimensional universe where time is the fourth dimension). Massive objects, such as the sun, curve the fabric of space-time around themselves as they move, much as a human cannonball dimples a safety net. Seen that way, the planets don't orbit the sun because a gravitational force holds them onto elliptical paths (as Newton predicted). Instead, each planet travels along a straight line (a geodesic), but its path is elliptical because it is moving in curved space.

Although several critical aspects of the theory remain untested, it appeals to cosmologists because it is the most elegant way to explain the behavior of many massive objects moving at velocities close to the speed of light. General relativity is used, for example, to explain the way black holes and active galactic nuclei warp space around them, and the way light is bent as it travels through large gravitational fields. "There's no issue of the *Astrophysical Journal* that goes by without an implicit reliance on the theory of general relativity," says Stuart Shapiro, a theoretical physicist at Cornell University whose specialty is general relativity and who is a strong backer of Gravity Probe B.

Yet it has always nettled those who rely on the theory that it has been so difficult to test. Einstein himself could think of only a couple of small effects to test, such as observing the way Mercury's orbit processes as it spins around the sun—gradually turning in its plane through an angle minutely different from Newton's prediction. Stars observed near the edge of the sun should appear slightly displaced outward, while light leaving a star should change color subtly, shifting toward the red. By now, these errors have been largely confirmed, yet not everyone is willing to conclude from this success that Einstein was therefore entirely right. In fact, physicists such as Nobel laureate C. N. Yang have predicted that Einstein's theory will break down at some point, partly because the mathematical structures for it and quantum mechanics seem utterly incompatible. One place to start looking for such a breakdown is to search for some of the more profound phenomena described by general relativity: For example, no one has directly observed the existence of gravitational radiation—the undetected waves of energy that travel through space, exerting gravitational forces on any mass in their path.

Even less is known about another phenomenon predicted by general relativity: frame dragging. This notion holds that a rotating massive body, such as a black hole or Earth, slowly drags space-time with it as it spins. It was just this concept that particularly interested Schiff. The Stanford researchers realized they could line up gyros on a distant star and then see if Earth's rotation would drag space and time around with it and alter the direction of the gyros' spin. If Newton was right, the gyroscopes should stay aligned on the star forever because there would be no effect of the spinning Earth. But if Einstein was right, Earth's rotation should drag space-time along with it, subtly altering the gyros' direction of spin over time. Schiff calculated that the instruments should be pulled out of alignment by a tiny angle of 42 milliarcseconds a year; Gravity Probe B aims to measure this change in spin to a precision of 1% or better.

To give you an idea of just how precise this angle is, it's like trying to see a fraction of the width of a human hair from 10 miles away. Which is why the main challenge that Gravity Probe B had to overcome over these last 30 years was for scientists and engineers to develop no less than four near-perfect gyroscopes that could do their job suspended in mid-air in a near-perfect vacuum at near-zero temperatures in near-zero-gravity in a near-zero magnetic field. All that effort is designed to protect the gyros from disturbances that could accidentally alter their spin: vibrations from the satellite, drag as the vehicle moves through tenuous gases, or accelerations caused by changes in solar radiation pressure.

Furthermore the satellite, which will have its position fixed by a telescope set on the guide star Rigel, 300,000 light-years away, will have to sense when the unmarked gyros' spin changes ever so slightly—and communicate that precise information back to Earth. Finally, there has to be a calibration system to make sure the instrument is free from errors that might masquerade as a relativity signal. No wonder Parker says, "This is a technical tour de force."

With Schiff as a senior adviser (until his death in 1971) Fairbank, Cannon, and Everitt put their heads together and also enlisted the help of other faculty and students at Stanford. The team came up with a closetful of technical wizardry: the world's roundest gyroscopes, a drag-free satellite, a refrigerated capsule capable of holding superfluid helium in place and cool for 2 years, and a method for detecting the change in gyro spin with superconducting technology. By 1984 NASA had decided the experiment should be tested on the shuttle, and Everitt and Parker selected Lockheed Missiles & Space Co., to help them develop the flight instrument.

Still, in the very face of this remarkable technical innovation, there has been a residual skepticism at NASA. The agency sent team after team to Stanford to examine the project—with many of those teams beginning as skeptics. Yet they all wound up recommending that the project go ahead. "Some of the best experimentalists have tried, but they haven't been able to poke a hole in it," says Shapiro, director of the CfA. "In the 25 years since I first reviewed it, Everitt and associates have showed that, by golly, it could be pulled off—if you're as clever as they are," adds University of Chicago physicist Parker. And for that reason, Parker's committee recommended this spring that NASA go ahead with the mission—but that it continue to leave the experiment in the hands of the team at Stanford, "It must be done precisely properly," says Parker. "If you put it in the hands of someone who is not as finely tuned, it probably won't work."

It may be a sign of the times, but in spite of such ringing scientific endorsements Gravity Probe B has barely escaped the budget-cutting knife. In fact, NASA and the Office of Management and Budget have separately axed the project in 1980, 1985, and 1990. The Senate Appropriations Committee also almost cut it this past August. Why would they cut this effort? NASA deputy administrator James R. Thompson—who says he would like to see it fly— concedes that it is an "elegant piece of science" but adds the usual explanation: Severe budgetary pressures caused the agency to make painful choices among an array of top science missions.

And in that kind of bureaucratic bloodletting, Gravity Probe B was likely to come out as a lower priority because it is "a sort of stand-alone thing," says Thompson, that doesn't fit in the usual mission categories, such as astronomy, observing platforms, or life sciences. Furthermore, Thompson says, it "doesn't have the broad constituency that the astronomy missions do"—meaning the experiment will be built and used by only one university, not many, as some projects are.

Despite these hammer blows, Everitt always revived his project, partly with the help of NASA insiders such as Charles Pellerin (head of astrophysics and physics) and researchers at NASA's Marshall Space Flight Center. "I did what people usually do after they've been zeroed. You learn to lobby," he says. Two congressional aides gave Everitt and Fairbank a crash course, and they took to the halls of Congress—learning to peddle the romance of Einstein, the glamour of high tech, and the value of educating students (the project has produced 33 Ph.D.s). Stanford even published a glossy 28-page brochure on the experiment.

The work paid off each time when Congress restored Gravity Probe B to NASA's budget. By now the project "has significant congressional support," says a staff member of the Senate Appropriations Committee. "It's good science, it's affordably priced, and it's not the kind of science that NASA usually supports. We think it would be a real tragedy to cut it." Obviously, so would the researchers at Stanford, more than one of whom has made it his life's work. "If I had known how long it would take when I started this at age 28, I would have thought I was a fool to have gotten into it," admits Everitt. But as Gravity Probe B stands now—with NASA funding, a launch date, and an enviable technological track record— Everitt can still add, "I am delighted that I did."

Reprinted with permission from Ann Gibbons, "Putting Einstein to the Test—In Space," SCIENCE 254: 939–941. Copyright 1991 AAAS.

On April 20, 2004, the dream of Leonard Schiff and his group of Stanford scientists was finally realized when Gravity Probe B was launched from Vandenberg Air Force Base in California. Gravity Probe B will measure two parts of Einstein's general theory of relativity: how the presence of Earth warps space and time and how Earth's rotation drags space and time. Released on September 7, 2004, this status report from NASA provides an update on the Gravity Probe B mission. —HH

"NASA Gravity Probe B Mission Enters Science Phase, Ready to Test Einstein's Theory"
by NASA
Marshall Space Flight Center Web Site,
September 7, 2004

Gravity Probe B (GP-B), a NASA spacecraft to test two predictions of Albert Einstein's general theory of relativity, achieved a major milestone this past week with the completion of the Initialization and Orbit Calibration (IOC) phase of its mission and the transition into the science phase. The GP-B mission is now one step closer to shedding new light on the fundamental properties of our universe.

"This is the moment we have been waiting for," said Francis Everitt, GP-B science Principal Investigator at Stanford University. "It represents a magnificent effort by the entire Stanford-NASA-Lockheed Martin team."

The GP-B spacecraft was launched on April 20, 2004 from Vandenberg Air Force Base, Calif., aboard a Boeing Delta II expendable launch vehicle. For the past four months, GP-B has been orbiting 400 miles above Earth, completing system checkouts and fine-tuning one of the most sophisticated science instruments ever put in orbit. On August 27 the spacecraft began science data collection.

"It's been a long, amazing road to get to this point," said Rex Geveden, deputy director of NASA's Marshall Space Flight Center in Huntsville, AL. "When Gravity Probe B was first proposed more than 40 years ago, the technology required for this experiment did not yet exist. At least nine new technologies had to be invented and perfected, with the program's advances only possible through breakthroughs in cryogenics, drag-free satellite technology, and new manufacturing and measuring technologies."

The spacecraft uses four ultra-precise gyroscopes to test two extraordinary predictions of Einstein's 1916 theory that space and time are distorted by the presence of massive objects. Specifically, it is testing two effects: 1) the geodetic effect—the amount by which the Earth warps local spacetime in which it resides, and 2) the frame-dragging effect—the amount by which the rotating Earth drags local spacetime around with it.

"It's great to be in our science mode," said Gaylord Green, GP-B Program Manager at Stanford University. "The team is ecstatic that the demanding IOC phase is over and the science phase has begun. Most importantly, all systems are meeting or exceeding the requirements of the mission."

At launch, the spacecraft's Dewar (the largest ever put in orbit) contained approximately 650 gallons of superfluid helium—enough to maintain the gyroscopes in a cryogenic state for an estimated 16 months. The GP-B mission time line originally specified two months for initialization, checkout, and instrument tuning, 13 months of relativity data collection, and one final month of instrument re-calibration. The IOC phase actually required a little over four months to complete. Although this results in a slightly shorter data collection period than originally planned, GP-B will significantly surpass its mission performance requirements.

Tuning up the Attitude and Translation Control system to achieve the extraordinarily precise pointing and drag-free positioning requirements of the spacecraft, as well as refining the set-up up the science gyros, accounted for the IOC extension. "These are items that cannot be tested on the ground," said Gaylord Green. "Using the extra time required for the checkout phase, the team obtained invaluable information about the GP-B science instrument."

The science phase is the heart of the GP-B mission. During this phase, at least twice a day, data is relayed from Earth-based ground stations or NASA's data relay satellites to the GP-B Mission Operations Center at Stanford University in Stanford, Calif. This data includes space vehicle and instrument performance information, as well as the very precise measurements of the gyroscopes' spin-axis alignment relative to its guide star, IM Pegasi. Over the course of a year, the anticipated spin axis drift for the geodetic effect is a minuscule angle of 6,614.4 milliarcseconds, and the anticipated spin axis drift for the frame-dragging effect is even smaller, only 40.9 milliarcseconds. This angle is so small that if someone were to climb a slope of 40.9 milliarcseconds for 100 miles, he would rise only one inch in altitude, measured to an accuracy of better than 1/100th of an inch.

The GP-B mission has already achieved many extraordinary accomplishments:

- GP-B is the first satellite ever to achieve both 3-axis attitude control (pitch, yaw, and roll), and 3-axis drag-free control (while orbiting the Earth, the whole spacecraft flies around one of the science gyros).

- The GP-B gyros, which are performing perfectly in orbit, will be listed in the forthcoming edition of the Guinness Book of World Records as being the roundest objects ever manufactured.

- The spin-down rates of all four gyros are considerably better than expected. GP-B's conservative requirement was a characteristic spin-down period (time required to slow down to ~37% of its initial speed) of 2,300 years. Recent measurements show that the actual characteristic spin-down period of the GP-B gyros exceeds 10,000 years—well beyond the requirement.

- The magnetic field surrounding the gyros and SQUIDs (Super-conducting QUantum Interference Device) has been reduced to 10^{-7} gauss, less than one millionth of the Earth's magnetic field—the lowest ever achieved in space.

- The gyro readout measurements from the SQUID magnetometers have unprecedented precision, detecting fields to 10^{-13} gauss, less than one trillionth of the strength of Earth's magnetic field.

- The science telescope on board the spacecraft is tracking the guide star, IM Pegasi (HR 8703), to superb accuracy, and it is also collecting long-term brightness data on that star.

The GP-B program will *not* release the scientific results obtained during the mission until after the science phase has concluded. It is critically important to thoroughly analyze the data to ensure its accuracy and integrity prior to releasing the results.

NASA's Marshall Space Flight Center manages the GP-B program. NASA's prime contractor for the mission, Stanford University, conceived the experiment and is responsible for the design and integration of the science instrument, as well as for mission operations and data analysis. Lockheed Martin, a major subcontractor, designed, integrated and tested the space vehicle and built some of its major payload components.

Courtesy of NASA.

3

Using Telescopes to Study the Universe

The following article from Laser Focus World provides a short history of the telescope. Telescopes are one of the main tools that astronomers use to explore the universe. When most people think of telescopes, they think of visible light, or optical, telescopes. In fact, the first telescopes to be constructed and used to study space were optical telescopes. The two main kinds of optical telescopes are refractors and reflectors. The earliest telescopes were refractors, which used lenses (like eyeglasses) to collect and focus light. Reflecting telescopes use mirrors to focus light. All of the major astronomical telescopes that are built today are reflectors. Author Thomas Higgins describes the development of both of these types of telescopes and introduces the important figures behind early telescope design, including Galileo Galilei, Hans Lippershey, Johannes Kepler, James Gregory, Isaac Newton, and Guillaume Cassegrain. —HH

From "Telescopes: All Eyes on the Skies"
by Thomas V. Higgins
Laser Focus World, February 1995

From the earliest spyglasses to the latest orbiting observatories, optical telescopes have broadened our window on the universe.

In 1610, Galileo Galilei (1564–1642) published an extraordinary booklet, The Starry Messenger, in which he detailed his historic observations of the heavens through a new optical instrument. "I do not doubt," wrote Galileo, "that in the course of time, further observations will improve this new science." If only he were alive today to appreciate the full extent of this understatement.

After nearly four centuries of improvements, telescopes continue to revolutionize our view of the cosmos. And just as in Galileo's time, much of what astronomers see through today's instruments still baffles them. In fact, astronomy has recently entered into a tumultuous era of discovery largely stimulated by a modern renaissance in telescope technology (see Laser Focus World, Dec. 1993, p. 50). But it was Galileo who inspired the first optical revolution in astronomy, and he did it with a spyglass of his own making.

As much as Galileo wanted his benefactors to believe he invented the first telescope, it was actually the Dutchman Hans Lippershey (ca. 1570–1619) who first applied for a patent on the device in the fall of 1608. By the time Galileo heard about the invention nine months later in Venice, the first telescopes were being sold as toys in Paris and Thomas Harriot was already mapping the moon's surface with one in London. Based on what he had heard, Galileo successfully constructed his first telescope in August 1609, and by March of 1610 he published his now famous booklet.

Galileo's first telescope consisted of two lenses mounted inside a lead tube. The first lens, called the objective, is convex and would normally form a real image of a distant object at the focal point (F_O) were it not for the second lens. The second lens, which is called the ocular or eyepiece, is concave and lies in front of F_O by one focal length (f_E). In this configuration, the real image that would normally form at F_O becomes a virtual object for the concave eyepiece to magnify. The final image presented to the eye is enlarged by an amount equal to the negative ratio of the two focal lengths, $-f_O/f_E$, where f_O defines the focal length of the objective.

In September of 1610, German astronomer Johannes Kepler (1571–1630), who was fascinated by Galileo's spectacular successes in Italy, completed a theoretical treatise in which he attempted to explain the principles behind the refracting telescope (refractor) using geometrical optics. Kepler called the work Dioptrice (from the Greek "to see through"), and in it he included an optical description of another type of refractor. Because of Dioptrice, this other refractor has become known as tile Keplerian astronomical telescope and all retractors are generically referred to as dioptric telescopes.

Like Galileo's telescope, Kepler's telescope uses an objective and an eyepiece to magnify the image of distant objects, but the eyepiece is convex instead of concave. With this design, the eyepiece must be placed one focal length behind the focal point F_O in order to magnify the real image of the objective. This lengthens the telescope. As with the Galilean telescope, magnification of the final image equals the negative ratio of the two focal lengths, $-f_O/f_E$. But the existence of a real image at F_O makes the Keplerian telescope a more versatile optical design.

The most obvious difference between the two instruments is that Kepler's telescope produces an inverted image and Galileo's does not. This difference is of little concern when viewing astronomical objects, but for terrestrial observations it is crucial. The upright image partly explains why Galileo's telescope contributed so much to his fame and fortune. In fact, the compact optical design is still used today in opera glasses.

But with additional optics, Kepler's astronomical telescope also can deliver an erect image if needed. For example, adding a third convex lens between the objective and the eyepiece forces the light through two focal points, F_O and F_E, which essentially inverts the inverted image. But this makes the telescope considerably longer. Another method, which does not add extra length, uses inverting optics such as the Porro prism or Pechan prism. Binoculars, which usually consist of one Keplerian telescope for each eye, use these prisms to create an erect image.

The chief advantage of the Galilean and Keplerian telescopes, however, is their light gathering power. This, of course, defines the raison d'etre of any astronomical telescope. The quantity of light collected by a refractor is proportional to the area of the objective. Galileo's first telescope had an objective with a diameter of roughly 2 in.; therefore it gathered more than 60 times the light of a dilated human eye. With that kind of light-gathering power, Galileo could see stars that no one had ever seen before, and this changed forever the ancient science of astronomy.

As Galileo had predicted, further observations through refractors led to many more technical improvements. Higher magnifications for studying extended celestial objects such as the moon, sun, and planets were accomplished by fabricating longer-focal-length objectives and shorter-focal-length eyepieces. Long-focal-length objectives with spherical surfaces of unequal curvatures also helped minimize spherical and chromatic aberrations. Chester Hall's invention of the achromat in 1733 finally eliminated the bothersome chromatic aberrations of objectives. And multielement eyepieces were created for higher magnification, fewer aberrations, and a wider field of view.

Refractor Limits

But while these and other advances established the refractor as a premier optical instrument for astronomy, there were practical limits to how large these telescopes could be made. The fundamental problem is that the light-gathering element of a refractor is a lens. Not only must each surface of the lens conform to its prescribed shape within a fraction of a wavelength, but the lens material must be highly transparent and homogeneous, too—free of bubbles, striae, and impurities. As Joseph von Fraunhofer (1787–1826) discovered, this is very difficult to achieve with large-aperture objectives.

Even with the highest-quality glass, though, very large objectives sag under their own weight, distorting the optical surfaces differently as the telescope is pointed in different directions. The world's largest working refractor, located at Yerkes Observatory in Williams Bay, WI, has an objective 40 in. wide, which is just about the limit. But the largest refractor ever built, the Great Paris Refractor of 1900, contained an objective with a diameter of 1.25 m. This gigantic telescope had a focal length of 60 m and was permanently mounted on its side to prevent shifting mechanical stresses on the objective. A flat, 2-m movable mirror relayed light from the sky to the objective.

Reflecting Telescopes

In the quest for more light-gathering power, the Great Paris Refractor stands as an ironic reminder of why today's most powerful telescopes use mirrors instead of lenses to collect the light. With mirrors, the transparency and optical homogeneity of the material are of no concern—only the quality and shape of the reflective surface matter. Mirrors also have no chromatic aberration and can be made much larger than lenses.

Many of the advantages of reflecting telescopes (reflectors) were realized early on by men such as James

Gregory (1638–1675), Isaac Newton (1642–1726), and Guillaume Cassegrain. But because the mirrors of these early telescopes were made of heavy speculum metal, astronomers had to wait until the invention of light-weight, silvered glass mirrors (after 1856) before the reflector could begin its rise to ascendancy. Although it was probably the Franciscan friar Marin Mersenne who first suggested the reflector in 1636, Gregory proposed a practical optical design in 1663.

The Gregorian reflector gathers light with a large concave mirror, called the primary, polished into the shape of a parabolic. All of the light reflected from the primary passes through the primary focal point F_P and illuminates a small concave mirror called the secondary. The secondary mirror, which is polished as an ellipsoid, redirects the light through a hole in the primary to the secondary focal point F_S, where an eyepiece then magnifies the image.

Newton, however, was apparently the first person to actually construct a reflector in 1688. Like the Gregorian, the Newtonian telescope uses a concave parabolic primary, but before the reflected light reaches the primary focus, a flat secondary mirror diverts it through a hole in the side of the telescope tube. An eyepiece then magnifies the image that forms at the secondary focus.

Cassegrain's design, which appeared at about the same time as Newton's, resembles the Gregorian telescope, except that the secondary mirror assumes the shape of a convex hyperboloid. The secondary intercepts light from the parabolic primary before it reaches the primary focus, which makes the telescope more compact than the Gregorian.

In spite of Newton's contemptuous assertion that "the advantages of this device are none" the Cassegrain design forms the basis of most modern telescopes.

On a clear night in the country, far from the city lights, you can see about 3,000 stars with your naked eye. With a pair of binoculars, the number of stars you can see increases to tens of thousands. With a medium-sized telescope, you would be able to see hundreds of thousands of stars. With a large observatory telescope, millions of stars would be visible to you. As you can see, when it comes to telescopes, size does matter. Big telescopes are better than small telescopes because they are able to collect more light. In the following article from Time, several large telescopes—including Hale, Subaru, Gemini North, the twin Kecks, and the Very Large Telescope (VLT)— are described. Among other things, these "glass giants" help scientists search for extraterrestrial planets. In the last decade, they have been used to detect numerous planets revolving around nearby stars. —HH

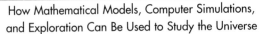
"Beyond Hubble"
by Michael D. Lemonick
Time, November 13, 2000

The sun is setting over the luxury resorts of Kona, on Hawaii's Big Island. Warm tropical breezes drift lazily through the palms. Honeymooning couples sip mai tais by the pool as waves break gently on white sand.

Just 30 miles inland, conditions aren't quite so pleasant. The sunset is every bit as gorgeous from here, at the summit of the long-dormant volcano Mauna Kea, but temperatures hover around 38°F, with a windchill that dips well below freezing. At an altitude of nearly 14,000 ft., the atmosphere carries barely half the oxygen it does at sea level, so the slightest exertion can leave visitors gasping. Those who travel to the summit without getting properly acclimated risk altitude sickness and even death.

But with night skies that rank among the clearest and darkest on Earth, Mauna Kea offers an unsurpassed view of the heavens—and that's why, despite the harsh conditions, astronomers can't wait to visit. Stargazers come here from around the world to answer some of the deepest mysteries of the cosmos: When in the depths of time did galaxies first flare into existence, and what made it happen? What is the elusive dark matter whose mass dominates the universe? How many stars have planets—and do those alien worlds harbor intelligent life?

Those questions and more have tantalized astronomers for decades—and Mauna Kea is one of the few places where answers may finally be found. The mountain is dotted with white and silver observatory domes, sprouting like oversize mushrooms from the barren, rocky rubble that was once molten lava and, much later, a holy place of the native Hawaiian people. And although it's not obvious to the casual visitor, these domes conceal stargazing machines of unprecedented power.

For nearly a half-century, starting in 1949, the world's most powerful research-quality telescope was the Hale, on Palomar Mountain, in California. Its mirror, 5 m (17 ft.) in diameter, focused more faint starlight than anything else on the planet. But in the past few years, the Hale has been humbled. Here on Mauna Kea alone sit the Subaru telescope (no relation to the car), with a mirror more than 8 m (27 ft.) across; the Gemini North telescope, also topping 8 m; and the kings of the mountain, the twin Keck telescopes, whose light-gathering surfaces are an astonishing 10 m—33 ft—in diameter.

The story is the same all over the world. In the high Andes of northern Chile, five more 8-m-class telescopes are either finished or nearing completion, while peaks in Arizona, Texas and South Africa too boast scopes more powerful than anything known to science just a decade ago.

That's not all. While each of these instruments trumps the Hale in light-gathering power many are poised to outshine even the Hubble Space Telescope, which has been delivering astonishing snapshots of deepest space since it was refurbished in 1993. The orbiting observatory's nearly 2.5-m (8-ft.) mirror isn't all that powerful, but since it floats above Earth's constantly roiling atmosphere, the Hubble has been unrivaled in the sharpness of its images. No more. Using an ingenious technological trick to eliminate atmospheric blur, most of the new telescopes will soon achieve Hubble-quality focus—and even beat it under the right conditions.

This is a breakthrough of astronomical proportions. Whereas for years scientists have had only one Hubble quality telescope, they will soon have access to more than a dozen. "What's been happening in the telescope game," says John Huchra, a veteran observer and a professor at the Harvard-Smithsonian Center for Astrophysics, "is incredible."

It has also been a long time coming. Impressive as the Hale telescope was for its day, it represented a technological dead end. The Hale, like its smaller predecessors, was powered by a mirror that's essentially a huge hockey puck of glass ground into a concave, light-focusing curve on one face and coated with reflective metal. To keep from sagging under its own weight and distorting the curve, the mirror had to be a bulky 26 in. thick and it weighed 20 tons. That enormous heft called for an even more massive support structure to hold the whole thing up while at the same time adjusting constantly to counteract the effect of earth's rotation. Scaling the design up any further would have been absurdly expensive.

During the 1960s astronomers' lust for light was temporarily satisfied by the development of electronic light detectors. Because these detectors are up to 100 times as sensitive as photographic plates—the standard recording medium since the turn of the 20th century—every telescope on Earth saw its power boosted a hundredfold essentially overnight. That kept the scientists happy only for a while, however, and everyone agreed that telescopes needed some sort of radical new design. Unfortunately, says Matt Mountain, director of the Gemini Observatory, "nobody knew how to make the conceptual leap."

By the early '80s, though, telescope designers were leaping all over the place. University of Arizona astronomer Roger Angel's solution to the sagging-glass problem was to cast huge mirrors that are mostly hollow, with a honeycomb-like structure inside to guarantee stiffness. University of California at Santa Cruz astronomer Jerry Nelson opted instead to create a mirror not from a single huge slab of glass but from 36 smaller sheets that would, under a computer control, act as one. And in Europe, design teams come up with yet another idea, the exact opposite of Angel's; instead of making the mirror hollow to save weight, let it be thin—about 8 in. thick for an 8-m mirror, in contrast to the 5-m Hale's 26 in.—and counteract the resulting floppiness with computer-controlled supports that continually readjust its shape.

"People argued at the time that it would be crazy to rely on computers because they might fail," recalls Mountain, whose Gemini telescopes in Hawaii and Chile ware built on the European model. "But when you think about it, planes are controlled by onboard computers, and those computers essentially never fail."

Neither do the ones that run the telescopes. The European Southern Observatory's New Technology Telescope, built in the 1980s as a 3.5-m precursor to the Very Large Telescope (VLT), worked beautifully. So did Keck 1 when it went into operation in 1992. And so, in turn, have the other big telescopes as they've come online over the past two years. With both enormous size and smooth performance, these giant telescopes are doing science on a heroic scale—especially the Keck, which has had more than a half-decade head start on its rivals. In fact, says an astronomer who prefers to remain anonymous lest his outspoken views earn him professional enemies, "The Keck has done way more science over its lifetime than the Hubble."

He may be right. The Hubble's forte is taking brilliantly sharp pictures. But the real meat of astronomical discovery comes not so much in pretty photos of celestial objects but in the detailed analysis of their light. By smearing that light into a spectrum—the rainbow of its component colors—scientists can identify the chemical makeup of a star or galaxy, how far away it is and how fast it's rotating, among other data. If the image of a star is going to be smeared anyway, sharp pictures don't matter much, so ground-based telescopes are at no disadvantage.

So while the Hubble is good at locating faint celestial objects, the follow-up science is often done by observatories on the ground. In essence, the Hubble is like the small finder telescopes backyard astronomers use to pinpoint interesting objects for their full-size telescopes.

In many cases, though, the ground-based giants can find their own way through the universe. Geoff Marcy, for example, leader of the world's most prolific planet-hunting team, began his research at the relatively modest 3.5-m telescope at Lick Observatory in California. Then, in 1996, he moved most of his project to the Keck, with dramatic results. We've discovered 35 planets orbiting sunlike stars so far," says Marcy, who holds joint appointments at the University of California, Berkeley, and San Francisco State University. "And the majority of them have been with the Keck."

The objects Marcy looks at aren't especially faint: he and his collaborators find planets by looking for stars that wobble under the gravitational tug of unseen companions. But the wobbles are so subtle that a lesser telescope can barely detect them. "With a 10-m telescope," says Marcy, "we can look at fainter stars and pick out the signature of smaller objects."

Indeed, Marcy announced last year that he'd found a planet the size of Saturn—the smallest yet discovered. "We think we can get down to the level of Neptunes," he says, "which are only 10 times as massive as Earth." Despite having so many planets in hand, Marcy and other astronomers haven't found anything like our home solar system: most of the planets found elsewhere are not only huge, but they career around in orbits that would fling smaller, Earth-like planets out into space— a discouraging start to the search for life in the galaxy, though it's far too early to give up.

George Djorgovski is using the Keck as well, but where Marcy's quarries are no more than 200 light-years away, Djorgovski's are closer to 10 billion. A professor at Caltech, Djorgovski has lately been concentrating on gamma-ray bursts—mysterious flashes of high-energy radiation that have baffled astronomers for nearly 40 years. If these blips of electromagnetic energy can be seen from far across the universe, as some astronomers believe, then they must briefly shine as bright as the rest of the stars in the universe put together—a seemingly preposterous assertion.

But in 1998, Djorgovski and his colleagues used the Keck to take visible-light pictures of a burst first spotted by the Compton Gamma Ray Observer satellite—and sure enough, it came from billions of light-years away. To date, the best explanation theorists have come up with is that the bursts come from "hypernovas," massive stars exploding with hitherto unsuspected power. "I feel really fortunate," says Djorgovski. "This was a world-class mystery, and the Keck allowed us to help solve it."

UCLA astronomer Andrea Ghez, meanwhile, has focused her attention on the center of our home galaxy, the Milky Way, far closer than Djorgovski's gamma-ray bursts but hundreds of times farther away than Marcy's planets. Shrouded in thick clouds of dust, the galactic core is invisible to ordinary light detectors. But among the Keck's suite of specialized instruments is an electronic camera sensitive to infrared light—the same kind of invisible light that your remote control uses to communicate with your TV. Infrared light of some wavelengths can penetrate dust as though it weren't there, giving Ghez a perfect view of the Milky Way's core.

Armed with the combination of the Keck's power and the detector's sensitivity, Ghez has been able to measure the motions of stars that lie 100 times as close to the core as the nearest star, Proxima Centauri, lies to the sun, and she finds that they're whipping around the galactic center at 1,600 miles per second, nearly 100 times as fast as Earth orbits the sun. It only takes high school physics to calculate that the object they're orbiting is as massive as 3 million suns yet packed into an area no bigger than the orbit of Mars.

The only thing that reasonably fits this description is a black hole, an object whose gravity is so strong even light can't escape from it. "We have evidence of these supermassive black holes in several other galaxies," says Ghez, "but this is the most convincing case we know of."

With their six-year head start, the Kecks have done more science than the newer telescopes, but the newcomers haven't wasted any time catching up. The European Southern Observatory's VLT, for example, built and operated by a consortium of eight countries, got the first of its four 8.2-m telescopes up and running in 1998 and achieved "first light" with the fourth in September.

But it's already doing first-rate science. Earlier this year, for example, astronomers from Sweden, Italy, Denmark and Germany used one of the scopes to help solve astronomy's so-called age paradox. In the mid-1990s, astronomers used the Hubble to measure the age of the universe at between 8 billion and 12 billion years. But other experts insisted they knew of stars that were at least 14 billion years old—obviously a problem, since stars can't be older than the cosmos. Using the VLT, though, observers have measured minute traces of radioactive uranium and thorium in the oldest stars—a technique akin to radiocarbon dating—and proved that they're more like 12 billion years old (the age of the universe, meanwhile, is now estimated at 14 billion years).

In fact, whereas the Europeans started later than their American competitors, they could pull ahead before too long. Not only do they have four giant telescopes on one site, but they've also budgeted more money than anyone else for state-of-the-art light detectors.

Still, U.S.-based telescopes remain ahead on several fronts, including the detwinkling of starlight. The technology that does this is called adaptive optics, and it was originally developed in secrecy by the Department of Defense to help military snoops take sharp pictures of Soviet spy satellites. Largely declassified in the 1980s, it's now being adapted for major telescopes everywhere. The idea is straightforward: stars and galaxies twinkle and shimmer because turbulent pockets of air act as weak light-distorting lenses (heat rising from a car's hood or an asphalt parking lot causes a similar effect). With adaptive optics, though, a computer can measure the shimmer and cancel it out.

Adaptive-optics systems do have limitations. To start with, they work well only with infrared radiation. That's not a huge problem, given that infrared is ideal for spotting new planets and for studying the early universe, the core of the Milky Way and the formation of stars. A bigger drawback is that adaptive optics can currently correct only for a small patch of atmosphere at the center of the telescope's field of view. But pockets of atmospheric turbulence are small enough that a slight change in viewing angle means a whole different pattern of distortions, which in turn requires a different pattern of corrections.

Even with these limitations, astronomers at both the Keck and Gemini have taken pictures that are every bit as clear as the Hubble's. Clearer, in fact, because a large telescope's images are inherently sharper than a small one's. Indeed, Ghez's latest and sharpest Keck images of the galactic center have been made with the adaptive optics.

Will adaptive optics make space telescopes obsolete? Not entirely. Space is still the best place to take supersharp pictures by ordinary light. And some radiation—ultraviolet, for example, and some wavelengths of infrared—can't penetrate the atmosphere at all. Moreover, telescopes radiate infrared light of their own, which contaminates celestial images. That's why NASA's plan to launch a Next Generation Space Telescope by 2009 still makes sense. With an 8-m mirror of its own, NGST will be able to see distant galaxies, for example, that no earthly telescope could ever see through the glare of its own heat.

Adaptive-optics systems may sound complicated, but they pale beside another technological trick that will ultimately boost telescopes' power even more. Called interferometry, it achieves the precise focus of a

truly huge telescope without actually having the thing
built. Instead, light is combined from widely separated
telescopes—the two Kecks, say, whose observatory
building was designed with a basement-level chamber
for that purpose, or two or more of the four VLT telescopes in Chile. The system is dauntingly tricky and
complex, but its astonishing precision will let
astronomers tease out the details of galactic structures
and distant solar systems as never before.

Yet even this remarkable technology could become
obsolete—along with the giant telescopes on Mauna
Kea, Chile and everywhere else—if the grandiose plans
of the world's astronomers come to pass over the next
couple of decades. Telescope designers are already
thinking about the next generation of ground-based
supergiant telescopes, devices that will range in size
from 30 m (100 ft) across to staggering 100 m, or 330
ft—a telescope mirror wider than the length of a foot-
ball field. These will probably be scaled-up versions of
the Kecks, using hundreds of individual mirrors aligned
to make a single giant that could have up to 100 times
the Kecks' light-gathering power.

Armed with a new generation of adaptive-optics systems now under development, these futuristic scopes
will once again revolutionize astronomy. "When we were
planning for the Keck in the early days," recalls Caltech's
Djorgovski, "we laid out some of the science we expected
to do with it. And we were much too conservative: we
missed most of the really important stuff we've actually
found. I predict the same thing will happen with these

enormous telescopes. We'll almost certainly find things we never could have imagined."

Telescopes that detect invisible bands of light in the electromagnetic spectrum have come about only in the last half century. Scientists have designed telescopes to detect wavelengths from across the electromagnetic spectrum: radio waves, microwaves, infrared waves, ultraviolet waves, X-rays, and gamma rays. After discovering that other bands of light existed, scientists then had to figure out how to detect and collect these photons that they were unable to see. The following article from Communications News *describes how the Arecibo Observatory, a radio telescope in Puerto Rico, collects, magnifies, records, and analyzes radio waves from throughout the universe. Many celestial objects, such as pulsars and active galaxies (like quasars) produce large amounts of radio-frequency radiation. Radio telescopes like Arecibo assist in our understanding of the universe by making these objects "visible" to us. Because of this, the Arecibo Observatory has become a favorite destination of many of the world's top astronomers. —HH*

"Reach for the Stars"
by Scott Stevens
Communications News, **December 1999**

Tucked away in a natural depression in the northern mountains of Puerto Rico is the Arecibo Observatory, the world's largest radio-radar telescope, part of the National Astronomy and Ionosphere Center. The observatory's mission is to detect and analyze electromagnetic (EM) radiation reaching the earth's surface from distant sources.

The success of Arecibo comes in part from being the planet's largest curved focusing antenna and, thus, the most sensitive. The centerpiece is a main reflector dish which measures 1,000 feet in diameter and covers about 20 acres. A 900-ton platform structure is suspended 426 feet in the air directly over the main dish. Three massive towers set around the perimeter of the dish provide support for the suspended platform. The tension of the support cables is constantly monitored to provide stable positioning so that, under normal wind loads, the platform moves only a fraction of a centimeter.

The complexity of this endeavor is best illustrated with radio astronomy. The Arecibo telescope must listen to the universe's "static noise" and collect and magnify that "noise" a hundredfold. The amplified signal is then sent from the receive site on the antenna platform to the control room in the base building 2,000 feet away where it is recorded and analyzed. It is paramount for accurate data analysis to keep the original signal pure, untainted with extraneous noise. Thus, the entire data-collection and communication system must be super sensitive yet not impart or accept any noise into the signal path.

A sophisticated network design has been developed by the engineers at Arecibo. To capture the incoming EM radiation, a carriage house on the trackable arm holds very sensitive and highly complex radio receivers. The receivers operate in a bath of liquid helium to maintain receiver temperature at 16 degrees above absolute zero (-459 Fahrenheit). At such cold temperatures, electron noise in the receivers is nearly nonexistent and only the incoming signal is amplified.

The amplified signal is then sent through specially designed filters and switches that select and isolate a specific wavelength range of the incoming radiation. (Arecibo can detect incoming radiation at wavelengths anywhere between 50 MHz and 10 GHz.) The filtered radio frequency (RF) signal is then transmitted via fiber optics to the base station for analysis. While fiber often is considered a digital medium, the fiber optic system employed at Arecibo transmits signals directly at RF frequencies and in their original analog form. This minimizes the equipment required at the carriage house while simultaneously providing high-performance, low-noise operation.

To achieve such a high fidelity, Arecibo chose Ortel Corp.'s "linear fiber optics." This analog system uses distributed feedback (DFB) lasers to generate an optical signal that is directly, or "linearly," proportional to the input electrical signal. At the other end, an optical receiver converts this modulated light back to the original electrical signal. DFBs were chosen because they provide the lowest noise and highest linearity of any semiconductor optical sources and are able to maintain the fidelity of the original signal.

For the optical cable, Arecibo chose a 56-fiber, stranded loose-tube cable (20 single-mode and 36 multimode) manufactured by CommScope, Inc. The singlemode fibers in CommScope's loose-tube design provide high bandwidth and extremely low attenuation which is critical for AM transmission where the signal-to-noise ratio (SNR) determines the signal quality. If the SNR is degraded by the cable, crucial data can be lost.

Along with stringent transmission parameters the cable needed to be rugged enough to withstand the harshness of the outside plant environment. The high heat and humidity of Puerto Rico can age fibers rapidly without protection. The loosetube cable provided by CommScope provides four layers of defense—polyethylene jacket, gel blocking, buffer tubes, and another layer of gel blocking within the tubes—protecting the fibers from moisture ingress. In addition, the CommScope cable decouples the fibers from the cable strength elements. This strain-free design prevents the fibers from experiencing stress either during wide temperature swings (i.e., jacket expansion/contraction) when the cable is under tension. Without this decoupling feature built into the cable, strain on the fiber can increase its attenuation and cause signal loss or disrupt data.

The sensitivity of the antenna system cannot be overstated. During operation, even small amounts of terrestrial noise can be picked up by the antenna and thwart system readings. To prevent unwanted EMI [electromagnetic interference] from leaking into the readings, the office and housing structures at Arecibo have been built with EMI shielding. Portable electronic devices, such as cellular phones, are not allowed on the premises. Even automobiles with electronic fuel-injection systems are prohibited beyond guest parking. To further isolate noise sources, Arecibo is planning to re-cable its entire LAN system with fiber optics.

While single-mode fibers are used for the receive-signal data channels, multimode fiber is used at Arecibo for system monitoring and controls, such as antenna positioning and radar transmission. Fiber is also used to monitor and adjust the cable tiedowns that keep the 900-ton platform virtually motionless. Even the tension on the reflector dish must be monitored and adjusted to prevent it from changing shape as temperature fluctuates and wind blows.

In addition to performance, reliability is another critical factor for the system. Scientists must schedule in advance critical time periods to collect data. In some cases, they may have to wait nine months more for certain celestial bodies to become viewable. During their often brief periods on site, everything must work flawlessly. While there is scheduled maintenance that is ongoing, the fiber system has never failed—even during a recent hurricane that swept through the island.

The observatory is always in the process of being improved in the quest for greater sensitivity and expanded capabilities. Now, with its state of-the-art data-collection network in place, and a new Gregorian horn antenna, Arecibo will continue to be on the cutting edge of space exploration, acting as a magnet to draw the world's leading scientists to do what can't be done anywhere else on earth.

Reprinted with permission from *Communications News*.

Astronomers use many filters in their work. Filters help astronomers analyze particular wavelengths of the spectrum by blocking out others. For example, a red filter successfully blocks out all visible light except that which falls around 600 nanometers (which is the wavelength of red light). Unfortunately for astronomers, Earth's atmosphere acts as a filter, blocking out most wavelengths in the electromagnetic spectrum. This makes it difficult for telescopes to collect certain bands of light. This problem can be partially alleviated by placing observatories high on mountaintops where the air is thin and dry. However, the best viewing location is by far in outer space. In this article, science writer Warren E. Leary introduces us to a space telescope known as Sirtf, or the Space Infrared Telescope Facility. In 2003, Sirtf was successfully launched into space. (Shortly after the launch, it was renamed the Spitzer Space Telescope). During its two-and-a-half-year mission, it will send back to Earth information to help us

understand our cosmic roots and how galaxies, stars, and planets form. —HH

"The Cosmos Gets Another Set of Eyes"
by Warren E. Leary
New York Times, **April 8, 2003**

NASA is preparing to launch the last of its "Great Observatories," space telescopes that astronomers hope will explore the faint warm glow of the early days of the universe and see through the billowing clouds of interstellar dust that obscure the birthplaces of stars and, possibly, far-off planets.

The telescope, a robot observatory that the space agency calls the Space Infrared Telescope Facility, or Sirtf, is scheduled to be launched on April 18 from the Cape Canaveral Air Force Station on a Boeing Delta II rocket. Sirtf (pronounced SIRT-ef) will travel in an unusual orbit: It trails the Earth from a distance on its mission to map the infrared, or heat, emissions from objects near and far.

Sirtf is the last in a suite of space telescopes that the National Aeronautics and Space Administration proposed in the 1970's. The idea was to place them above the obscuring atmosphere of Earth and examine the heavens across the entire electromagnetic spectrum of light, ranging from gamma rays, X-rays and ultraviolet light on one end to infrared and radio waves on the other.

In the middle of this continuum is the small visible spectrum that includes the array of colors that the human eye can see. This is where the first and best known of the great observatories, the Hubble Space Telescope, does its work, writing itself into astronomical history by producing a continuing series of images that has given humans a new view of the wonders of the universe.

Sirtf is to follow the path charted by its companion orbiting observatories, which include the Compton Gamma Ray Observatory and the Chandra X-Ray Observatory, in mapping its special part of the skies.

"When the history is written of the latter 90's and early part of this century, the field of astronomy will he remembered for the contributions of the 'Great Observatories,'"the associate administrator for space science at NASA, Dr. Edward J. Weller, said. "We have realized our early goals with the observatories, and in about every case, we've exceeded our expectations."

Dr. Weller said no one telescope or instrument could look across the whole spectrum of light to study all aspects of the cosmos.

"Doctors don't examine you with one instrument," he said. "Astronomers studying the universe are doctors in that sense. They can't just look at the light seen by the eye and hope to understand what is happening out there."

Hubble was launched in 1990. Shortly afterward, a defect was discovered in the main mirror, threatening its effectiveness. It was repaired in 1993, when a space shuttle crew installed corrective lenses. Since then, it has been upgraded to keep it at the forefront of visible astronomy until it ends its mission in 2010.

Compton, launched in 1991, ended its successful mission in 1999 and burned in the Earth's atmosphere.

But before its demise, it discovered powerful bursts of gamma rays exploding from sources across the universe and studied other extremely high-energy phenomena like quasars, cosmic ray interactions and solar flares.

Chandra, launched in 1999 and scheduled to operate at least through next year, is studying sources of powerful X-ray emissions like black holes and big exploding stars known as supernovas.

Dr. Robert P. Kirshner, an astronomer and a professor of science at the Harvard-Smithsonian Center for Astrophysics in Cambridge, Mass., said the Great Observatories were having major effects on astronomy, scientifically and sociologically.

The observatories encourage cooperation among scientists who specialize in studying particular wavelengths of light, Dr. Kirshner said, because coordinated observations of the same phenomenon can show more than narrower studies. NASA also has more requests for observing time on each telescope than it has available. So astronomers are encouraged to pool objectives to yield more from each set of observations, experts said.

Dr. Kirshner said the model established for using Hubble, with a separate research institution set up to review proposals and distribute the information obtained, has also helped the field of astronomy. The Hubble model established the practice of giving astronomers who were allotted time on the telescope the money to analyze the information, he said, giving a needed infusion of scientific financing to astronomy.

"Hubble was really the key to making the Great Observatories program a success," Dr. Kirshner said.

"Its images got people interested in astronomy and made people understand that we are seeing something that is different and exciting out there. This also helped move interest forward in ground-based astronomy."

Dr. Anne L. Kinney, director of the astronomy and physics division at NASA headquarters, estimated the cost of the Great Observatories at $10 billion to design, build, launch and operate over their lifetimes. Most of that money, $7 billion, has gone to Hubble.

"There is no question that space telescopes are more expensive than ground observatories," Dr. Kinney said, "But if you can do what you can't do on the ground, it is worth it."

Scientists submit 1,000 proposals a year to use Hubble, with about one in seven accepted. About 800 proposals have been submitted for Sirtf, and many of those will have to be declined also, she said.

"This desire to use them is a true test of how valid the concept of the space telescope is," Dr. Kinney said.

The designs for Sirtf have been changed several times since 1979, when it was first proposed. At one point, it was to be a telescope based on the space shuttle; at another, a giant $2 billion rocket-launched telescope that orbited Earth like Hubble.

Cost overruns and technical challenges with infrared detectors further delayed the project, until NASA agreed to the scaled-down $740 million observatory.

Scientists and engineers said the delays helped the project, because new technical concepts came along that made the telescope smaller but more powerful than originally planned. The project benefited from advances in lightweight optics and developments with infrared detectors sponsored by the military, which uses similar sensors on to monitor Earth-based missile launchings from space.

The solar-powered Sirtf, which weighs about a ton at launching, measures 14.6 feet long, 6.9 feet in diameter and 5.25 feet deep. It was built by Lockheed Martin Space Systems, while Ball Aerospace and Technologies designed and built the telescope assembly. Ball also built two of the three scientific instruments on the observatory. The Goddard Space Flight Center of NASA constructed the other.

The observatory, designed for a mission of two and a half years that could stretch to five years, has two curved mirrors to gather and distribute infrared light, a primary mirror 33 inches in diameter and a smaller secondary one, each made from the ultralight, but strong, beryllium.

Anything in the universe with temperatures above absolute zero—zero degrees Kelvin or minus 460 degrees Fahrenheit—emits some heat, or infrared radiation. Because the heat of the telescope itself can obscure the readings, in a phenomenon called infrared noise, the observatory and its instruments have to be extraordinarily cold.

On earlier infrared satellite missions, the entire telescope and its detectors were encased in a giant freezer bottle containing a superchilled liquid-gas coolant. To reduce size and weight, the Sirtf designers took a radically different approach.

Just the chamber for scientific instruments and a compact coolant bottle with 95 gallons of liquid helium coolant will be cold at launching. Engineers are counting on the rest of the spacecraft to cool on its own in deep space to about minus 400 degrees, a process that will take about a month. Designed to take advantage of passive natural cooling, the Sun side of Sirtf is entirely shielded by its solar power panel, and that side of the spacecraft is a shiny silver color, to reflect heat. The opposite side is painted black to radiate residual heat into space.

To avoid heat contamination from the Earth and Moon, Sirtf will be placed in orbit around the Sun at a distance closely matching that of Earth's from the Sun. The spacecraft will trail in Earth's wake millions of miles away, but close enough to stay in contact with its science center at the California Institute of Technology in Pasadena.

"Sirtf," Dr. Weller of NASA said, "will allow us to complete the picture of the universe that the other Great Observatories started."

Using Computer Simulations to Investigate the Universe

4

It has been said that a picture is worth a thousand words, but what about an interactive virtual model of the universe? Computer modeling provides a vast array of new and exciting ways to learn about our universe. As our understanding of the universe increases, we gain a better idea of what it actually looks like. Since we cannot yet jump into a spacecraft and explore other star systems, we are, at the moment, mainly restricted to exploring the distant universe with telescopes, such as the ones featured in chapter 3 of this book. However, computer simulation and virtual reality compensate for this by allowing us to simulate the space experience.

The following article from a 1998 issue of Science News discusses the ability of cosmologists to create, for the first time, a computer model of the entire universe. With this new technology at their disposal, astronomers are prepared to make important new discoveries. —HH

"Modeling the Whole Universe"
by Ron Cowen
Science News, **July 4, 1998**

They've got the whole world in their computer. For the first time, cosmologists have harnessed enough computing power to model the entire observable universe. Beginning 1 billion years after the Big Bang, when the cosmos was almost perfectly smooth and uniform, the simulations trace the action of gravity as tiny fluctuations in density of matter that develop into a spidery network of huge filaments and voids.

The models depict the growth of huge clumps of matter over volumes of space hundreds of times bigger than the largest new telescope surveys will examine. Indeed, the project previews the biggest structures that the Sloan Digital Sky Survey and other huge surveys may discover, says August E. Evrard of the University of Michigan in Ann Arbor.

Astrophysicists believe that stars and galaxies comprise but a small fraction of the cosmos. The vast majority of matter is thought to be in some invisible, undescribed form called dark matter. The new simulations follow a type of slow-moving dark matter, cold dark matter, whose ability to gather into clumps is believed to hasten the formation of galaxies. Unlike ordinary matter, which is sensitive to electromagnetism and other natural forces, dark matter is influenced only by gravity.

Previous simulations had tracked the development of some 2 million chunks of dark matter, each millions of times larger than the most massive galaxies. These models painted with so broad a brushstroke that they could not portray details of the cosmic structures. Evrard came up with the idea of running more accurate simulations by using in parallel all 512 workstations of one of the most powerful supercomputers, located at the Garching Computing Center of the Max Planck Society in Germany. It took a year of preparation and months of running time for an international team of scientists known as the Virgo Consortium to perfect the models.

In a second set of simulations developed by the consortium, cold dark matter takes a back seat to the energy associated with the cosmological constant (SN: 5/30/98, p. 344). This term in Einstein's equations of general relativity acts to accelerate the expansion of the universe. Recent observations of distant supernovas and the clustering of galaxies support the existence of the cosmological constant. A preliminary analysis of the new model shows an abundance of distant, massive clusters, in good agreement with the observations.

Evrard notes that none of the simulations show the locations of clusters of galaxies or other luminous material, although such objects are often assumed to form within the densest concentrations of the dark matter. To directly incorporate galaxy formation, the models would have to include effects other than gravity, notably gas pressure, heat, and radiation.

The new models are "a stunning technical tour de force," says Richard Mushotzky of NASA's Goddard Space Flight Center in Greenbelt, Md. "Researchers have been struggling for many years now to model the [entire] universe . . . Whether it changes our understanding of the universe or not, we just don't know yet."

The technology used by astronomers has come a long way since the days of Galileo and Kepler. Today, sophisticated computers are indispensable in the field, assisting astronomers with a variety of tasks. Computer modeling, in conjunction with accurate observations, is an invaluable tool for studying and gathering information about the universe around us. Computer simulations allow astronomers not only to investigate places that would otherwise be unreachable, but they also simplify the task of solving difficult astronomical calculations. Thanks to computer models, the calculation of thousands of orbits, which used to be a difficult feat, can now be completed in as little as an hour by a single astronomer. The following article from Natural History explains how astronomers used computer simulations to predict and interpret the fate of the comet Shoemaker-Levy 9, which orbited Jupiter and eventually crashed into the giant planet. —HH

"The Virtual Universe"
by Mordecai-Mark Mac Low
Natural History, February 2000

A half-mile-wide pile of gravel and dirty snow hurtles past Jupiter, barely evading the grasp of its gravity. Still, the comet (for that's what this pile of debris is) begins to drift apart because of the feather-light difference between Jupiter's gravitational force on its near and its far sides. This tidal force strews pieces of the comet through space until they span a distance greater than the separation between Earth and the Moon. During the following year, bits of rubble from the ill-fated comet gravitationally reassemble themselves into a chain of twenty smaller objects. As Jupiter's gravity asserts itself once more, drawing the whole chain back toward the planet on an even more perilous orbit, astronomers on Earth finally notice that the comet is on a fatal course.

With the whole world watching, the first object in the chain plunges into Jupiter's atmosphere at more than 100,000 miles per hour, becoming the mother of all meteor strikes. Falling beneath the ammonia clouds that form the visible surface of the planet, the comet fragment vaporizes in the white-hot heat of its shock wave, releasing the energy of thousands of nuclear bombs. On Earth, the resulting fireball would stretch from New York to Chicago. On Jupiter, it blows material clear out of the atmosphere but is nevertheless a mere pinprick to the giant planet.

To predict, and eventually to interpret, the violent fate of comet Shoemaker-Levy 9 in July 1994, astronomers turned not just to their traditional tools— mathematical calculations and telescopes—but also to computer models. Computer modeling began just over half a century ago, initially driven forward by the race to design and build atomic weapons. Astonishing increases in computer speed and memory have since made it into a third method of scientific investigation, distinct from mathematical theory and from experiment and observation—yet relying on both.

In June 1993, soon after word of the comet's potentially catastrophic fate began to circulate among astronomers, Kevin Zahnle, of NASA's Ames Research Center, called me to suggest that we actually begin a collaboration we'd often discussed, one that would combine his knowledge of asteroid and comet impacts on planets with my expertise in astrophysical shock waves. The first moves were made not by us, however, but by dynamical astronomers, who used one of the most fundamental mathematical descriptions of the physical universe: the law of gravity.

Mathematical computations of the orbits of objects under the influence of both a planet and the Sun draw on a body of work stretching back more than 300 years to Isaac Newton. By the early twentieth century, orbit calculations were already being carried out by computers, although the word "computer" then referred not to a machine but to a member of an arduous profession that, as it happens, offered almost the only way available at the time for women to participate in astronomical research.

These human computers could calculate single orbits but not the thousands necessary for constructing a model of a fragmenting and reassembling comet. Now, though, such a herculean task can be completed in an hour or two by a single astronomer, who can then compare many models with the observations so as to find the best match.

The programs that compute these orbits use the principles of high-school analytic geometry to represent the motions of thousands of comet fragments. At the beginning of the computation, each fragment is assigned a position in space using three coordinates, along with an initial velocity (in the case of comet Shoemaker-Levy 9, the fragments were initially distributed in a sphere with a diameter of just under a mile). Using the law of gravity, the program next computes the forces acting on each fragment—from Jupiter, from the Sun, and from every other fragment—in order to determine the direction and distance that each will travel over a very short time. The coordinates of the fragments are then changed to their new positions, and the time is advanced. The program then repeats these steps, using the new positions and taking into account the slightly different forces now acting on them because of their motion with respect to one another, to Jupiter, and to the Sun. Repeating this relatively simple procedure thousands or even millions of times allows the computation of the entire comet breakup.

Each of the particles in such a computer program might represent something the size of a boulder, as in the case of comet Shoemaker-Levy 9, but it might just as easily represent a star—or even groups of tens of thousands of stars. Simultaneous computations of the orbits of tens of thousands of such massive particles can demonstrate how galaxies develop their beautiful spiral arms. By initially placing the particles in a uniform, rotating disk and then computing their interactions, astronomers find that spiral arms form whenever the disk arrangement is even slightly perturbed, as a natural result of the gravitational interactions between the stars. Similarly, but on an even grander scale, computations of collisions between spiral galaxies show that mutual gravitational interactions disrupt the orderly disks and throw stars out in spectacular streamers tens of thousands of light-years long as observed in contorted objects such as the Antenna galaxy.

These same computational techniques have led to a revolution in our understanding of the large-scale structure of the universe and the process of galaxy formation. Models of this process begin with not tens of thousands but tens of millions of particles, distributed through a representative region of the universe almost uniformly, just as matter was distributed in the earliest centuries after the big bang. Each particle in the simulation now represents a mass of millions of stars—still a small fraction of the billions of stars in a galaxy. Modeling the orbits of these particles under the mutual influence of all the other particles in the region reveals that areas of slightly greater density attract more and more mass, eventually forming stars and galaxies, while areas of slightly lesser density empty out, forming cosmic voids that can still be observed today. When the models are started with initial conditions consistent with observations, the resulting cosmic web beautifully reproduces the distribution of galaxies that we observe in the universe today.

Gravity alone is sufficient for predicting the behavior of boulders and stars only so long as no other forces become as strong. In the case of comet Shoemaker-Levy 9 on its final plunge, however, the fragments screaming into the wispy outer reaches of Jupiter's atmosphere entered the realm of hypersonic gas dynamics. The basic laws of gas flow were described 200 years ago by Leonhard Euler, but it was not until the middle of the twentieth century that researchers developing rockets and nuclear bombs first carefully computed the properties of strong shock waves and massive explosions. (To this day, classified U.S. nuclear weapons development centers maintain the largest computers available for such computations, although research centers that are open to all scientists offer strong competition.) When the atmosphere gets dense enough, the pressure forces overwhelm the gravitational forces between particles and must be included in the model.

This is where Zahnle and I entered the picture. I had already computed, in other contexts, many models that included pressure forces. Gas pressure varies, so to compute its effects, a coordinate system is set up, and a grid of points is defined throughout the region. At each point on the grid, the local pressure, density, and velocity of the gas are noted. For the comet collision, I used a software package called ZEUS (written by Michael Norman and his colleagues at the National Center for

Supercomputing Applications) to set up a grid covering a small region of Jupiter's atmosphere, with a sphere as dense as ice (representing the comet) falling through the grid at many times the speed of sound.

Because gas flows away from regions of high pressure and toward regions of low pressure, the program computes how the gas at each point will move under the influence of gas at neighboring points over a very short time period. These motions are then used to determine how the gas properties stored at each point in the grid change over this short time. By repeating this computation thousands of times, we can follow the gas flow: the comet fragment drives a high-pressure shock wave ahead of it, while the rest of the atmosphere remains undisturbed until the shock wave hits it, heats it, and drives an explosive expansion.

Zahnle and I based our computations of the comet's impact on previous models I had done of the effects of multiple supernova explosions on the gas between stars in the disks of spiral galaxies. Although the distances in these models were tens of trillions of times greater than those in the comet impact, and the explosion energies even more extreme, the physical mechanisms were quite similar. I scaled down the distances from light-years to miles by some thirteen powers of ten (one followed by thirteen zeros), scaled down the explosion energies by even more (a factor of twenty-three powers of ten), and found virtually the same expansion of an explosion in Jupiter's stratified atmosphere that I had found in the galactic models.

When interpreting computational models, we must always keep in mind two questions. The first is, Does the model contain all the important physical processes? Short of including not just every atom but every electron and photon, modeling always involves estimating how strongly different processes contribute to the situation and then deciding which processes can safely be ignored. For example, in my models of the comet impact, I neglected radiative heating of the icy comet fragment by the white-hot shock front below it, because of calculations by colleagues suggesting that radiative heating would be slightly less important than heating from the hot, shocked gas. Including the radiative heating would also have made the problem far more difficult to compute—always a consideration in deciding what to ignore.

The second question is, Does the numerical model actually simulate the physical processes we've decided to include? If the sampling, for example, is too coarse, important features can be missed, but if the sampling is too fine, the time needed for computing the model will be prohibitive. The question of how much sampling is enough arose during my computations of the comet impact. I realized that some of the first published models of the impact did not have fine enough grids to follow the way the comet was torn apart by the pressure forces. Instead, the fragments in these models remained intact and therefore punched much more deeply into the atmosphere, burying their energies and leading to predictions of less spectacular explosions.

Because of these two constraints, computational simulations can never stand on their own, independent of observation. The seeming completeness of simulations can easily seduce us into believing that they give a true picture of reality. Poor approximations or inaccurate numerical methods, however, all too often yield attractive but incorrect models. Only the interplay between model and observation can yield reliable information about the universe around us.

How will astrophysical computer modeling develop in the next decade? Computations of straightforward three-dimensional gas dynamics at moderate resolution are still a recent addition to the computational scientist's tool kit.

Now the challenge is twofold: first, to include more of the relevant physical processes, such as the chemical behavior of gas as it is heated to millions of degrees by hypersonic shock waves and then cools down almost to absolute zero; and second, to increase the resolution of the models so that, for example, the formation of individual galaxies can be followed in cosmological simulations.

The new generation of supercomputers presents its own challenges. Rather than being very fast single processors, they consist of hundreds or even thousands of off-the-shelf microprocessors linked by very fast communications networks. Programming these machines requires that all these individual units be coordinated without their generating the kind of internal traffic jams that clog the Internet. Another direction being pursued for increasing computational speed is the development of specially designed chips that can perform the most time-consuming parts of the simulations rapidly, so that desktop processors can achieve supercomputer speeds for particular types of problems. This technique has already proved particularly fruitful for particle simulations such as those described above.

Finally, the never-ending struggle to win insight from computation will depend not just on better simulations but also on better analysis of the results of those simulations. These analyses will more and more rely on computing how the results would appear if the physical situation simulated were observed through a particular telescope, and then comparing these simulated observations with real observations by that telescope. Increasingly, astrophysicists will attempt to understand complex observations with complex computer models, but always with the ultimate aim of gaining an understanding of the universe that can be confirmed by comparisons with observations of the real world.

What happens when one black hole collides with another black hole? Scientists are attempting to answer this question by studying gravity waves. Though the collisions of other astronomical giants, such as galaxies, produce light and radiation, the merging of black holes produces only invisible waves called gravity waves. As predicted by Einstein's theory of relativity, the

invisible waves ripple through the fabric of space-time but remain undetected. The following article written by scientists at the Max Planck Society explains how astronomers are attempting to use computer simulations to model the gravity waves that result from the merging of two black holes. —HH

"Computer Simulations Predict What Astronomers Will 'See' with Gravitational Wave Telescopes When Two Black Holes Collide"
by the Max Planck Society
Science Daily, September 19, 2001

The merging of two black holes is one of the strangest occurrences expected in modern astronomy. Now physicists using the world's biggest computers have shown astronomers what to look for and have brought the first observations of these events much closer.

In a paper that is to appear in Physical Review Letters on Sept. 17, 2001, a team of young researchers at the Max Planck Institute for Gravitational Physics (Albert Einstein Institute in Golm, near Potsdam and Berlin, Germany) has predicted the gravitational waves that should be emitted when black holes plunge towards each other and merge. The team consists of John Baker (now at NASA's Goddard Space Flight Center in the USA), Bernd Brügmann, Manuela Campanelli, Carlos Lousto, and Ryoji Takahashi. They call themselves the Lazarus Team.

The most important result of the Lazarus simulations will be to provide gravitational wave astronomers with a set of templates which they can use to recognize the signals in the noise at the output of their detectors. The Lazarus simulations make predictions that are more detailed and more reliable than any before. The Lazarus scientists expect the gravitational waves to be stronger than previously accepted estimates.

Bernard Schutz, one of the directors of the Max Planck Institute for Gravitational Physics, observes: "The success of the Lazarus Project at the AEI comes at just the right time. Black hole mergers could provide the first-ever detections, which will be a landmark for Einstein's theory of general relativity. Numerically computed gravitational wave-forms will not only help us to detect and recognize waves from these events, but will help us to deduce from the observations the masses of the holes and their distance from us. Black hole mergers emit no light, radio waves, or X-rays. We can only detect them by catching their gravitational waves."

Previous simulations have not been able to follow the black holes through the whole merger event. Deep inside a black hole lurks a "singularity," a place where gravity gets huge. Computer simulations have had difficulty modelling the waves outside the hole at the same time as the inside.

The key advance by the Lazarus team at the AEI came when they combined two approaches, full numerical simulation for the essentially strong-field regime of the collision and an approximation method, perturbation theory, for computing the radiation from the resulting distorted single black hole. They cut off the full simulation before it went bad, and then used a different method that looked only at the gravitational waves outside the merged hole. Computers again had to calculate this radiation, but they could avoid the problems caused by looking inside the holes.

Reprinted with permission from the Max Planck Society.

Computer modeling is a very useful tool for examining rapid processes such as black hole formation and virtually undetectable changes such as a Doppler shift. Without computers, it is quite difficult to detect planets outside our solar system. This is because the stars around which they revolve are so bright that the glare drowns out the light that is reflected off of them. The only way to detect these extra-solar planets is to measure their effects on their parent stars. As a planet orbits a star, it periodically pulls the star closer to and farther away from Earth. The motion of the star affects the spectrum of light emanating from it. These shifts in the spectrum of light coming from the star are called Doppler shifts. By measuring the shifts in the star's spectrum of light over time, astronomers can detect the presence of a planet. However, the Doppler shift is so slight that it is virtually undetectable

without the use of a computer. The following article from Computerworld *describes how astronomers developed algorithms that would model expected Doppler shifts. By comparing the spectrum obtained from their computers with observed spectra, they were able to detect more than fifty extra-solar planets.* —HH

"University of California, Berkeley Scientists Develop Algorithms to Discover Extra-Solar Planets"
by Gary H. Anthes
Computerworld, June 3, 2002

"People thought we were a little crazy," recalls astronomer Geoffrey W. Marcy. "When we told them we were going to look for planets around stars, they'd kind of look down at their shoes and scuffle a little bit."

Finding planets outside of our solar system seemed next to impossible in 1984 when Marcy began his search. Planets at great distances are just too small and dim, compared with the stars they orbit, to be seen by even the most powerful telescopes. Indeed, Marcy worked for 11 years before finding one.

But the former skeptics don't stare at their shoes anymore. Marcy, director of the Center for Integrative Planetary Science (CIPS) at the University of California, Berkeley, has found 52 of the 86 known "extra-solar" planets. He has won a slew of prizes and medals for his work, and he may be the only astrophysicist ever to appear on the Late Show With David Letterman.

It has been known for years on theoretical grounds that a planet orbiting a star would cause a slight perturbation in the gravitational field of the star, producing a tiny shift in the spectrum of starlight emitted. The problem was that this Doppler shift is so slight that it's virtually undetectable. Marcy saw the solution not in better telescopes but in better computer software.

Marcy and a colleague, Paul Butler, developed algorithms and wrote 50,000 lines of code to model the expected Doppler shift, then used statistical methods to compare this "synthetic" spectrum with observed spectra. "We spent thousands of hours in front of computer terminals to write code to do various tasks," Marcy says. "There was nothing we could take off the shelf."

The model resulted in Doppler shift measurements of unprecedented accuracy, good enough to detect the passage of a planet between its star and Earth. "It's one of the most important discoveries of the last 100 years," says Frank Drake, chairman of the board of trustees of the SETI Institute in Mountain View, Calif.

Early in the project it took six hours of computer time to process the data from a 10-minute observation of one star. CIPS now uses 20 high-end workstations from Sun Microsystems Inc. to process the same data in about 10 minutes.

But Marcy had to invent ultra-efficient data reduction algorithms as well. "For many years we didn't have an algorithm that was good enough, but we could see ourselves slowly but surely improving," he says. "It was a trying period, to put it mildly."

"It's a textbook example of how to do science," says Drake. "Marcy was dedicated, he made careful measurements and was very careful in the analysis of the data. He knew from Day 1 it would be a long time before he got results, but he stuck with it."

Reprinted with permission from *Computerworld* and RMS.

The following article written by Robert A. Simcoe describes the use of telescopes and computers to study the vast expanses between galaxies, known as intergalactic space. According to Simcoe, a physicist at the Massachusetts Institute of Technology Center for Space Research, advances in observational techniques and computer modeling have allowed scientists to create a sophisticated picture of this seemingly empty space. Simcoe describes the current technology used by astronomers to observe the intergalactic medium and then interpret their observations. He then goes on to describe how astronomers used their interpretations to create a theory of how the universe was formed billions of years ago. Computer simulation is especially invaluable in this evolving field. By adapting to new observations, theories, and technologies, computer simulation helps us to understand more about our universe every day. —HH

"The Cosmic Web"
by Robert A. Simcoe
American Scientist, January/February 2004

There is no such thing as empty space. The idea of absolute emptiness realizes its closest approximation in the barren expanses between the stars and the galaxies, but even the most remote corners of the universe are suffused with very low density gas—which becomes increasingly rarefied as one ventures farther away from the places where galaxies consort. Consider this fact: In the air we breathe, each cubic centimeter contains roughly 5×10^{19} atoms. In contrast, the intergalactic medium has a density of only 10^{-6} particles per cubic centimeter—each atom inhabits a private box a meter on each side. This would seem to suggest that there is not much matter in the intergalactic medium. But, given the enormous volume between the galaxies, it quickly adds up: The combined atomic mass of intergalactic gas exceeds the combined atomic mass of all the stars and galaxies in the universe—possibly by as much as 50 percent! There is indeed something in empty space.

As cosmologists construct new narratives of the universe's evolution from its beginning—the Big Bang—to the present day, it is becoming clear that we must understand the physics of intergalactic matter if we are to write the history of how the galaxies, stars and planets formed. In the past decade, rapid advances in both the design of telescopes and computing power have allowed us to study the remote corners of intergalactic space in unprecedented detail. These new results deepen our understanding of how the grandest structures in the universe formed and evolved.

In the Red

Intergalactic gas is so tenuous and dark (producing no light of its own) that you might well ask how astronomers can hope to observe it. The trick is to detect it indirectly, by seeing how it influences light coming from faraway sources. The most common object for these observations is a quasar, a special type of galaxy containing a supermassive black hole at its center. Gas around the black hole emits intense radiation, which often outshines the average galaxy by 100 or more times. Because quasars are so bright, we can observe them at great distances and so measure the effects of intergalactic gas over substantial portions of the universe.

Using the world's most powerful telescopes, we can collect photons from these distant beacons and sort them by their wavelengths into spectra. The strongest feature in such a record is an emission line that is produced by hydrogen atoms near the quasar's black hole. The electrons in these atoms are excited to a single quantum level above their ground state. When they settle back to ground, photons are emitted with the precise wavelength of 121.56701 nanometers—called the Lyman-α transition. Yet we observe the emission line at a much longer wavelength, 560 nanometers. This is because the quasar is racing away from us, carried by the general expansion of the universe (see "The Hubble Constant and the Expanding Universe" in *American Scientist*, January–February 2003). The expansion is such that objects far from us recede proportionally faster than those that are close. As an object moves away from us, the light that it emits is stretched to longer wavelengths in much the same way that the Doppler effect lowers the pitch of a receding train whistle. Astronomers use the term redshift to describe this phenomenon, since the colors of ever-more-distant objects become systematically redder.

Now consider what happens to the light of a quasar when it is transmitted through the intergalactic medium. As light from the quasar heads toward the Earth, some of its photons will intercept hydrogen atoms along the way. If one of these photons has a wavelength of 121.56701 nanometers, it will be absorbed by the atom, which then has one of its electrons kicked out of the ground state. When the electron loses energy and falls back to the ground state, the photon is re-emitted, but in an arbitrary direction, which is not likely to be toward Earth. So a cloud of hydrogen atoms will absorb light at a very specific wavelength and scatter it away— we see this as a dark "hole" in the spectrum.

The intergalactic medium contains many hydrogen clouds at different distances from us. And because clouds at different distances have different redshifts, a quasar spectrum shows many absorption lines at different wavelengths. The wavelengths below the hydrogen emission line thus appear to be "eaten" away according to the location of each cloud between the quasar and us. In the past decade new instruments on large telescopes have allowed us to examine the spectra of quasars at very-fine-wavelength resolution and high signal-to-noise ratio. These "zoomed-in" views resolve the intergalactic medium into individual clouds.

Spinning a Cosmic Web

When the absorption lines of quasars were first studied, it was not at all clear how to interpret them, particularly without the benefit of the high-quality data we have today. From the late 1970s to the early 1980s, Wallace Sargent's team at Palomar Observatory made a series of measurements that convinced most astronomers that these absorption lines represent intergalactic matter. However, a number of theoretical explanations were consistent with the available data, and most models explained the lines as clusters of discrete spherical clouds of gas.

In recent years, the advances in observing techniques have been joined by increasingly powerful computer models, which together deliver a more sophisticated picture of the intergalactic medium. This work involves several collaborations and requires months of supercomputer time. In these simulations, an imaginary box is designed to resemble a large representative volume of the universe. The box is divided up into a three-dimensional grid of cells, and matter is distributed throughout the grid in an initial state—according to conditions set by observations of the early universe. All of the physical processes that affect the evolution of the intergalactic medium are dialed into the model. Then the simulation is "turned on," allowing matter and energy to flow from cell to cell in the box, governed simply by the physics. The final product resembles a cosmic time-lapse movie with millions of years compressed into each frame. The computer code examines the distribution of matter in the box at each frame, or time step, and calculates the total force acting on each particle to determine where it should move in the next step. At regular intervals, the computer records the density of the gas throughout the intergalactic medium, and these results are compared with actual observations of quasar spectra to test the accuracy of the physical models.

One such output [is] from a simulation run by Jeremiah Ostriker and Renyue Cen of Princeton University. This particular view shows the universe when it was about 15 percent of its present age, or about 2 billion years old. The most striking feature seen is a tendency for gas to collapse into a network of filamentary tendrils that crisscross through vast, low-density voids. This pattern is a common feature of the new computational models and has been nicknamed "the cosmic web."

To test this depiction of the universe against concrete observations, large numbers of artificial quasar spectra are generated by drawing random lines through the simulation box. By evaluating the variations of gas density along any single line, astronomers can calculate the amount of absorption that would be observed in a spectrum measured along that line of sight. It is as though an observer stood on one side of the box and measured the spectrum of a quasar on the other side.

Statistically, the "spectra" from these artificial universes are nearly indistinguishable from the spectra of real quasars. The models accurately predict the number of absorption lines, the distribution of their strengths and widths, and their evolution through time. At a basic level, these models have captured the physical processes that dominate the evolution of the universe on the largest scales.

Lumps and All

Technology has thus given us the tools to observe the remote corners of the intergalactic medium and to interpret these observations in the context of a cosmological model. Having described the methods, now let us step back to examine the model itself by offering a narrative that explains the formation of galaxies and intergalactic structure.

The story begins more than 13 billion years ago, roughly 380,000 years after the Big Bang, when the universe was very different from today. There were no stars, galaxies or webs yet, just a uniform soup of free-floating protons and electrons. In fact, the gas was so evenly distributed that its peak densities differed by only 1 part in 100,000 from the cosmic average. But sometime between then and now it evolved into a very lumpy place, where vast stretches of nearly empty space are interrupted by "dense" strands of galaxies and gas. Today, the range of densities is much greater: The difference between the atomic density of the Sun's interior and intergalactic space spans about 32 orders of magnitude!

Astronomers believe that this transition from smooth to lumpy was driven by gravity. Imagine a box containing a perfectly uniform distribution of matter, so that the density of the particles is constant.

Suppose that at one location in the box the particles are somehow stirred, leading to a slight density enhancement at this particular spot. This tiny new concentration of mass will create a gravitational force, which tugs on the surrounding particles and causes them to fall inward. The infalling matter increases the clump's mass, which in turn increases its gravitational pull, allowing it to assemble even more material, and so on. Given enough time, this "gravitational runaway" transforms what was originally a tiny density enhancement into a dense clump, containing most of the mass that was distributed throughout the volume.

This simple phenomenon is the basis for theories of how the large-scale structure of the universe was formed. Yet in order for it to work, the universe must have been "imprinted" at some earlier time with a network of primordial density perturbations that would later collapse into the structures we see today. As it happens, the signature of these ripples has been observed—as tiny variations in the temperature distribution of microwave photons coming from different parts of the sky. Characterization of this microwave background is currently a major focus of astronomical research, as the ripples represent the ancient gravitational seeds of cosmic structure.

It would seem that we have all the elements needed to explain the origin of the cosmic web. We have observed density variations in the early universe, and we have a powerful model that explains how they could evolve into larger structures. However, there is one problem: The primordial variations were so small that 13.7

billion years is still not enough time to grow them into the assemblages we observe today! This puzzle received a great deal of attention during the 1970s, perhaps fueled by Cold War politics. Two competing theories of structure formation emerged, one devised by Yakov Zel'dovich at the School of Russian Astrophysics in Moscow, and the other by James Peebles and his collaborators at Princeton University. The ensuing debate exposed significant weaknesses in both theories. The solution required the introduction of an entirely new ingredient—ominously named *dark matter*—in the cosmological models. This proved to be one of the most important discoveries in modern cosmology.

This dark stuff is quite different from the ordinary matter that makes up stars, planets and people. Not only does dark matter not shine, it interacts with "our" kind of matter only through the force of gravity. It is largely believed to consist of exotic particles that have no other effects on ordinary atoms and molecules. Furthermore, dark matter appears to outweigh normal matter throughout the universe by a factor of four to one. This notion is indeed odd, and it has met with resistance since it was first suggested by the eccentric astronomer Fritz Zwicky in the 1930s. However, cosmologists have now grown to accept its existence as nearly certain in the face of overwhelming evidence from a variety of observations. Although we may not understand exactly what dark matter *is*, we do understand what it *does*—it holds galaxies together, bends light, slows down the universe's expansion and drives the formation of intergalactic structure.

To understand this last point, we need to return to the early history of the universe. During the first 380,000 years, the relic heat from the Big Bang kept the universe so hot (greater than 3,000 kelvins) that electrons and protons in the primordial soup could not combine to form neutral hydrogen atoms. Such ionized gas, in this case consisting of dissociated electrons and protons, is known as a *plasma*. When plasma particles are in their free-floating state, they can interact with light, exchanging energy and momentum. In the early universe, this scattering increased the gas pressure within the cosmic soup. So, when gravity tried to collapse the first density perturbations, the gas pressure pushed back—much as a balloon does when it is squeezed. As long as the electrons and protons were separated, the gas could not form larger structures. Instead, the potential structures churned and oscillated as the inward pull of gravity fought the outward push of gas pressure.

Then, when the universe was 380,000 years old, a major event took place. As the universe was expanding, it was also cooling, and at this point it became cold enough for electrons and protons to combine, forming hydrogen atoms. Suddenly, these new atoms became decoupled from the photons—they no longer interacted so strongly with light—which drastically reduced the pressure that had kept gravity at bay. With gravity free to work on all the newly formed hydrogen atoms, structures could form in earnest.

How did dark matter fit into the picture? While the protons, electrons and photons were oscillating under the competing influences of gravity and pressure, the dark matter followed a different storyline. Because dark matter interacts with normal matter only through gravity, the pressure that kept the normal gas from collapsing couldn't act on it. Particles of dark matter enjoyed an unimpeded assembly into large structures long before the normal gas could begin to get organized. By the time normal matter decoupled from the photons, the dark matter had already grown into a primitive web-like network. As soon as the normal matter lost its support from the photon pressure, the gravity from the pre-existing dark-matter structures quickly pulled normal gas into the web. In this way, normal matter was given a gravitational "head-start" by the dark matter.

Once this process was set in motion, the gravitational building blocks of the intergalactic medium were in place. Normal and dark matter continued to free-fall toward concentrations of mass until the rising gas pressure slowed the infall. The web-like lattice was taking shape, but stars had not yet begun to form and all of the gas in the universe was neutral. The universe had entered an age where matter drifted about in the darkness, quietly assembling under gravity's influence. So it continued until at some point—probably somewhere between 200 million years and one billion years after the Big Bang—a process began that would fundamentally alter the nature of the intergalactic medium and the universe as a whole: The first stars were born.

Fiat Lux

It seems preposterous that something as small as a star could affect the universe on intergalactic scales. After all, a star is only a few light seconds across, whereas the filaments of the cosmic web may extend for billions of light-years. How can a relatively tiny object impact such a large volume? The answer lies in how stars work, where they live and what happens when they die.

Before there were stars, the normal matter in the universe was composed almost entirely of hydrogen and helium. Astronomers refer to this mixture as a chemically pristine gas because it reflects the chemical composition of the cosmos just after the Big Bang. Since then, nearly every atom of every other element—from argon to zinc—was forged inside a star. Stars are effectively nuclear fusion reactors: They gravitationally compress gas to such high densities that light atomic nuclei smash together to form heavier elements. Such stellar nucleosynthesis releases enormous amounts of energy, and that's what makes the stars shine.

Nucleosynthesis had several important effects on the intergalactic medium. First, it generated starlight, which escaped into intergalactic space and interacted with the neutral atoms. Later, the newly minted heavy elements were ejected into the intergalactic medium by strong *galactic winds*—powerful expulsions of hot gas—that stirred up and "polluted" vast regions of the universe.

Let's consider these processes in more detail by returning to the cosmic web. Because galaxies are more than 10,000 times denser than the cosmic average, we would expect to find systems like the Milky Way within dense regions of the web itself, which contain the raw materials (gas reservoirs) needed to build the stars and galaxies.

In simulations, the densest regions are found within the web's filaments, especially where several intersect. Therefore, on cosmic scales, galaxies should behave like tiny particles trapped in the strands of the web, actually tracing the much larger structures outlined by intergalactic gas. Recent three-dimensional galaxy surveys, such as the Sloan Digital Sky Survey and the 2dF Galaxy Redshift Survey, have indeed revealed a filamentary pattern in the way that galaxies cluster. Research groups, led by Max Tegmark at the University of Pennsylvania and Rupert Croft at Carnegie Mellon University, are currently investigating the clustering statistics of galaxies relative to those of the intergalactic gas as seen in quasar spectra. Their early results suggest that the same physics underlies the assembly of the intergalactic gas network and large-scale galaxy structures.

As the galaxies coalesced out of the web and began to shine, the universe was filled with the first new light since the Big Bang—the dark era had ended. And the stars dutifully began to churn out heavy elements. When enough stars had formed, the cumulative production of light and chemicals began to alter the nature of the intergalactic medium itself. Astronomers refer to these collective effects as "galaxy feedback," because the galaxies act on the surroundings from which they formed. Here I'll only consider two types of feedback, radiation and chemical pollution.

The first agent of galaxy feedback was starlight, which reionized the intergalactic medium. Recall that normal matter began to form large structures during the era of *recombination*, when the protons and electrons teamed up to form hydrogen atoms, so the gas in the universe was, for a time, entirely neutral. It was also very cold, reaching gas temperatures only a few tens of degrees above absolute zero. When the first stellar photons leaked out from galaxies, they interacted with the hydrogen atoms, stripping away the electrons that had been in place since the era of recombination and reheating the resulting plasma up to temperatures near 10,000 kelvins. Reionization was initially confined within bubbles centered on the fledgling galaxies, because the starlight had not yet traveled far out into intergalactic space. As more galaxies began to shine, the ionized bubbles grew outward until those from adjacent galaxies began to overlap. Soon the entire volume of the universe was once again ionized.

We now believe that the universe finally emerged from its "dark ages" and was reionized when it was less than 1 billion years old, or about 10 percent of its present age. Today, only about 1 hydrogen atom in 10,000 is in a neutral state and the average temperature of intergalactic gas is still very near 10,000 kelvins.

A Mighty Wind

It had long been assumed that the intergalactic medium was chemically pristine and that the production and distribution of new elements took place only within galaxies themselves. But astronomers also noticed that a few weak absorption features in quasar spectra appear redward of the hydrogen emission line. These other lines arise from different elements—carbon and silicon—whose characteristic wavelengths are redder (longer) than hydrogen's 121.56701 nanometers.

The absorption lines of these heavy elements are observed within regions that also contain a considerable amount of hydrogen. These zones correspond to gaseous halos around the first galaxies, whose stars were thought to supply the chemicals. However, in the early 1990s, quasar spectra taken by Lennox Cowie and Antoinette Songaila on the newly commissioned Keck telescopes revealed heavy elements far removed from any galaxy. Their discovery suggested that the chemical pollution of intergalactic space was much more efficient than originally believed.

The concentration of heavy elements in the intergalactic medium is very low: For example, only about one carbon atom can be found for every million (mostly hydrogen) atoms. So a box of intergalactic space that is 100 meters on a side would contain just a single carbon atom! Yet even this tiny amount reveals that some heavy elements were mixed throughout the cosmic web early in the history of the universe. How did they get out there—so far from the stars and galaxies in which they were made?

The evidence suggests that they were blown out into intergalactic space by violent *galactic winds*. These streams of matter flow out of galaxies where stars are actively forming. In all galaxies, the most massive stars burn brightly, and rapidly produce new elements. These stars burn so fast that they quickly exhaust their nuclear fuel and can no longer continue fusing light elements into heavier ones. When the reactor in a massive star turns off, the star ends its life in a tremendous explosion known as a supernova. The blast energy of a typical supernova rivals the simultaneous detonation of 10^{31} atom bombs, and the remnants of the dead star—including its newly fused heavy elements—are launched into surrounding space.

Despite its explosive power, a single supernova cannot pollute the intergalactic medium because the gravitational force from the star's galaxy traps the expanding debris before it can escape. However, galaxies occasionally experience bursts of unusually vigorous star formation where stars are born and die 10 to 50 times faster than usual. During these starbursts, multiple supernovae can be triggered in near succession. Their collective energy drives debris outward, like a rocket boosted by several stages, breaching the gravitational barrier and expelling heavy elements into the intergalactic medium. This phenomenon has been observed in a number of nearby galaxies.

Although we can study nearby starbursts and the resulting outflows in exquisite detail, these galaxies are the rare exception in the local universe. Most galaxies quietly go about forming stars and manage to retain the heavy elements they produce. But in the early universe, the situation was quite different. New observations of distant galaxies by Max Pettini at the University of Cambridge and his colleagues have revealed that outflows were extremely common when the universe was about 15 percent of its present age. This has two important implications. Nearly every galaxy we see today underwent some period of intense star formation in its past. And large quantities of heavy elements were launched into the intergalactic medium very early in the life of the universe. There was thus plenty of time for this material to coast out to large distances and mix with the chemically pristine intergalactic gas.

Studies of early galaxies and their feedback on the intergalactic medium define an important frontier of our knowledge about the first stars and cosmic structures. Several important questions remain open. For example, exactly when and where did the first stars form? Do heavy elements pervade the entire universe, or is there still chemically pristine gas left over from the Big Bang? Were the stars that triggered reionization the same stars that produced the observed intergalactic heavy elements?

For the past few years I have been investigating some of these questions with Wallace Sargent at the California Institute of Technology and Michael Rauch at the Carnegie Observatories. We have been measuring heavy-element concentrations in the early cosmic web to learn whether there are pristine corners of the universe that have not yet been reached by the galactic winds. So far we have detected heavy elements throughout all of the strands of the cosmic web, but it is still not clear whether the winds' sphere of influence extends beyond the filaments and into the intergalactic voids. In these remote regions the expected heavy-element densities are so low that even our most sensitive observations cannot reveal their absorption lines

directly. Nevertheless, our results show that debris
from galactic winds must have dispersed into most of
the mass in the universe before the cosmos was a mere
20 percent of its present age.

We have also compared our observations with different models of star formation and chemical
production to determine whether the stars that reionized the universe were the same ones that polluted the
intergalactic medium. Our results suggest that the earliest stars did not produce most of the heavy elements,
most likely because their heyday was too short. Instead,
we believe that galaxy feedback occurred in a series of
waves. The first generation of stars reionized the universe, and later generations progressively enriched the
intergalactic medium with chemicals.

On the theoretical front, the most advanced cosmological simulations are just beginning to
incorporate realistic models of galactic winds and the
chemical enrichment of the universe. The physics of
star formation and galaxy outflows is so complex that
even the most sophisticated numerical models must
make broad, simplifying assumptions to make the
problem computationally tractable. The subject continues to progress rapidly, as both the observations
and the theory evolve.

There are, of course, many details to be refined.
Exactly how and when did the first stars form? How do
galaxies and the intergalactic medium interact? And,
perhaps most importantly, what is the nature of dark
matter? Yet, when sufficient time has passed to offer a

historical perspective, the past decade may well be remembered for the emergence of a standard model of the cosmos that ties all we know about galaxies and the intergalactic medium into a single package.

Reprinted with permission from *American Scientist*.

5

Exploring the Universe Through Travel—The Space Program

The following article from Air Power History discusses the origin of the United States space program and particularly highlights President Eisenhower's Open Skies policy. In 1949, Americans learned that the Soviets had successfully exploded an atomic bomb. Fear that the Soviets would use the bomb against other countries began a period of mutual distrust between the United States and the USSR. During this Cold War period, the two countries battled over supremacy in space. This battle led to advances in the space programs of both nations. The world's first man-made Earth satellite, Sputnik I, was launched by the Soviet Union in 1957. Following the launching of Sputnik, the United States sprung into action, passing the Space Act of 1958, which ultimately brought about the National Aeronautics and Space Administration (NASA) and the National Aeronautics and Space Council (NASC). Since that time, NASA has been an invaluable tool for gathering information about the universe. —HH

"Open Skies Policy and the Origin of the U.S. Space Program"
by Lester F. Rentmeester
Air Power History, **Summer 2004**

In a 1946 speech at Fulton, Missouri, Britain's Winston Churchill declared that an "iron curtain" had descended over Europe to separate the East and the West. Indeed, by 1948, the USSR achieved control of Eastern European countries. When the Soviets exploded their own atomic bomb in 1949, it caused many in the U.S. to fear that they might use this weapon to achieve their expansionist ambitions. The period of mutual distrust and antagonism between the two nations could properly be called the forty-five-year Cold War.

Early in this period, President Harry Truman implemented the Truman Doctrine, asserting that Soviet aggression would be stopped at the northern boundaries of Greece and Turkey. My role in implementing this national policy was as an advisor to the Turkish Air Force, in developing their reconnaissance and intelligence capabilities.

In April 1950, President Truman ordered the National Security Council (NSC) to prepare NSC68, a policy paper authorizing major military force and expending up to 20 percent of our GNP, to meet a Communist threat anywhere in the world. Two months later, North Korean forces invaded South Korea. In his usual firm manner, Truman rallied United Nations forces to defend South Korea.

Upon my assignment to the Air Force headquarters in 1951, with responsibility for development of reconnaissance and intelligence systems, I learned of the high priority placed on defining Soviet strategic capabilities and intentions. That winter, the Air Force had procured the Beacon Hill Study in Project Lincoln at the Massachusetts Institute of Technology. Among the outstanding scientists at that time were James Killian, James Baker, and Richard Leghorn. Issued in June 1952, the Beacon Hill study reported on intelligence future forecasting. In research and development, the Reconnaissance Working Group was established in 1952. Its members worked closely with Beacon Hill. Because of the Air Force's major role in ICBM development and in strategic reconnaissance, the group's report was regarded highly. It stressed the fact that every nation's skies should be open for inspection of their military capabilities; their conclusions were stated in an Open Skies report.

Many other activities were aimed at divining USSR intentions. In 1947, the Air Force had established its Long-Range Detection Program to monitor the Soviet nuclear program. Its air-sampling capability discovered that the USSR had exploded a nuclear bomb in August 1949.

Detection devices of all types were gradually established around the Soviet Union. The National Security Agency was created in 1952, to gather communications intelligence (COMINT). Aircraft equipped with electronic gear gathered intelligence to determine the Soviet Union's air defense radar order of battle. Cameras, with very long focal lengths were installed in high-flying aircraft to photograph deep into the Communist bloc. Maj. Gen. George W. Goddard, the "father of aerial reconnaissance," who had survived five aircraft crashes since his pilot training in World War I, suffered his first injury, a broken leg, when he fell off a huge camera installed in a C-97.

In 1952, the U.S. exploded a hydrogen bomb device; the USSR tested their version the following year. The Air Force's Strategic Air Command (SAC), which had been established in 1946, had to be modernized and expanded. However, the Air Force did not have the resources for this until the Korean War liberated funding.

In response to the USSR atomic bomb, the Air Force needed intercontinental ballistic missiles (ICBMs) to destroy strategic targets. However, U.S. knowledge of the number and location of enemy targets, the input to ICBM guidance systems, and USAF charts were found to be grossly deficient. In March 1954, the Air Force Secretary Harold Talbott directed that the missile program receive all necessary funding. Development of the Atlas and Titan ICBMs, both with a 5,000-mile range, was stressed. The Thor, a 1,500-mile intermediate range ballistic missile (IRBM) was developed and tested rapidly—in less than four years—for use against closer targets. Gen. Curtis E. LeMay, SAC's commander-n-chief, insisted that the Pentagon provide the means to identify and locate the targets necessary to carry out his mission.

Fear of a surprise attack was so great that USAF commanders conducted reconnaissance overflights of the USSR's borders almost continually. When Gen. Nathan Twining was Air Force chief of staff, he claimed that he had forty-seven planes fly over the USSR at one time.[1] However, this type of reconnaissance (even if it was true) would not have provided the necessary intelligence on a possible Soviet missile and bomber in that nation's interior.

Some of our efforts to obtain information on Soviet capabilities and intentions bordered on the desperate. The Air Force took over a Navy research balloon project and attached to it a 1,400-pound camera package, so that it could take aerial photographs, while floating over the Soviet Union. When my boss, Maj. Gen. Donald Yates, was briefed on the project, he said that he thought that we were crazy, but authorized the $5 million to initiate the project. We soon found that winds at altitudes over 100,000-feet blew from east to west, instead of the westerlies found at lower altitudes. On our first flight to the west from Japan, the automatic timer released the camera package too soon and it fell in downtown Warsaw. However, enough of the 500 balloons used in the project blundered over some Soviet targets to make the project worthwhile. There were many other projects like this, some not as haphazard as the balloon program, as we in research and development tried to satisfy the SAC's need to define the Soviet threat. The two most promising projects for photo-reconnaissance were a very high altitude aircraft and a reconnaissance satellite.

In our efforts to develop long focal-length lenses, we had to create a new production process. Our best optics had been produced at an optical glass works in West Germany, but even they could not provide the huge

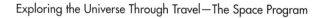

long-focal length optics that we wanted. This required a continuous flow-casting process involving close temperature control over a long distance. The major U.S. optics producers cooperated with the Air Force and other government agencies to solve the problem. During one step in the project, we borrowed a million dollars worth of platinum, needed for temperature control from the U.S. Treasury and transferred it to the Bureau of Standards for prototype testing.

Col. Joseph J. Pellegrini, who managed the reconnaissance research and development at the Air Research and Development Command (later called Air Force Systems Command), was the key figure in developing new programs. In August 1953, he initiated study contracts with Bell, Martin, Lockheed, and Fairchild for designs of a very high-altitude photo-reconnaissance aircraft. In an effort to keep the other military services from competing with us, he tied up all of the wind tunnel facilities in the United States with contracts to the Air Force. His office pursued an aggressive course with the major aircraft companies to produce designs for aircraft, satellite and component systems, even before we had sufficient funds and authority for hardware development.

It was a heady time for dreaming and scheming of ways to counter the Soviet threat. Col. Richard "Dick" Leghorn, a key figure in the USAF Open Skies group and Dr. Duncan MacDonald, another member, were gathering ideas from members of the scientific community. Those that we considered useful, we turned over to RAND Corporation, a USAF-funded think tank that had been studying the concept of an Experimental

World-Circling Spaceship, since 1946. One of our primary concerns during this period was the legality of using the skies over other sovereign nations for our purposes. We asked our think tanks, plus the experts at the Air Command and Staff School and the Air War College to produce studies on space law to justify our position.

As it turned out, when the USSR orbited the first satellite, nobody worried about space law any longer. The Soviets did protest in November 1960, that satellite photographs were illegal, no matter what the altitude from which they were taken. However, they soon developed their own electro-optical system, with real-time imaging capability.[2]

Colonel Pellegrini's request for proposals (RFP) for a one-man, high-altitude reconnaissance aircraft, which could operate at 70,000-feet altitude, went to four different aircraft manufacturers in August 1953. The competition resulted in the Bell X-16.

Meanwhile, in early 1954, the Air Force accepted the proposal submitted by Kelly Johnson of Lockheed because it would produce an acceptable aircraft in the shortest possible time. The U-2 (U for utility) aircraft was 63-feet long, had a 104-foot wing span, weighed 17,000 pounds, and could cruise at 430 miles-per-hour at an altitude over 70,000 feet for a 4,000-mile range. The photographic package in an interchangeable nose of the airplane was a 36-inch folded-lens camera designed by James Baker. Other interchangeable noses contained receivers of electronic intelligence, signal intelligence, etc. Although the wing-span of the U-2 was similar to the B-17 that I flew over Germany in World

War II, its powerful J57 engine, its light weight and its immense wing area were designed to take it to altitudes out of reach of the Soviet surface-to-air missiles.[3]

This high-altitude proposal was approved by Lt. Gen. Donald Putt, who was in charge of USAF development, Generals LeMay and Twining, and Air Force Assistant Secretary for R&D Trevor Gardner. When President Eisenhower was briefed in November 1954, he liked the concept but didn't want it to be a military project. Our Air Force briefer, Col. Paul Gremmler, told us that Ike said that he didn't want a blue-suiter (Air Force) pilot flying any missions and asked Allen Dulles, head of the Central Intelligence Agency (CIA) whether his outfit could do the job. That's how CIA got into the project and, incidentally, thwarted Pellegrini's plan to freeze out other agencies by tying up all of the wind tunnels. (Generals Twining and LeMay were so sure that the Air Force would take over the U-2 program that they furnished the $22 million dollars and 30 Pratt and Whitney J57 engines for the initial 20 aircraft.)[4]

Meanwhile, Col. Victor Genez in Pellegrini's office, worked with us in going to manufacturers to determine how the five subsystems, such as, propulsion, airframe, cameras, etc., could provide us with a workable reconnaissance satellite. Because of the constraints, we selected a television camera that would transmit its signal to three ground stations in the United States. This system led to the first project name, Feedback. Because of the low resolution of the images, the system was later discarded for this program although it was used a decade later in NASA's RANGER program. The Feedback

name for the project was changed often: SENTRY,
SAMOS, and PIED PIPER; KEYHOLE was the name
for various photographic systems, KH-1, KH-2, etc.

We used the RAND people to collect the ideas from
people concerned with the project. In October 1954,
they briefed my boss, Maj. Gen. James McCormack, and
others in the Pentagon. With General McCormack's
approval, I wrote a formal directive for the program, as
Weapon System 117L, Advanced Reconnaissance
System, requesting $12 million immediately and desig-
nating October 1956 as target date for the launch of the
first United States satellite.

Today, school children know about spacecraft; their
operation had to be explained to the five major generals,
heads of directorates, whose approval was needed for the
project because hundreds of millions of dollars would be
needed in future years. One asked me what held the
satellite up without wings. My answer used the example
of the moon as a satellite of the Earth and planet Earth
as a satellite of the sun. When I was explaining to
another about Keplerian motion and decaying orbits, he
said, "Do you mean to stand there and tell me that thing
will come back to Earth and probably hit me in the back
of the head when I'm not looking?"

At last the project was off and running. Lockheed
had the most responsibility for the reconnaissance
package and later replaced the TV camera with high
resolution optics in a system with high-pointing accuracy. In March 1955, Col. Gremmler wrote a General
Operational Requirement that further refined the system requirements in my WS-117L directive.

Briefings on the reconnaissance satellite, U-2 and a variety of other collection programs were presented to escalating levels of the Department of Defense and the CIA during the latter part of 1954. The CIA program director, who later was responsible for the Bay of Pigs operation, worked in coordination with the Air Force and Lockheed, resulting in the first U-2 flight in August 1955.[5] Colonel Pelligrini briefed the Joint Chiefs of Staff in December 1954, and the National Security Council received approval of the Open Skies Policy from Eisenhower in early 1955, following the Killian Committee's report in February. A few months later, at a superpower conference in Geneva in July 1955, Eisenhower proposed, as a step to prevent nuclear war, that nations give each other the right to use their airspace in an Open Skies Policy to prevent surprises. Nikita Khruschev was cool to his proposal.

At that time I was stationed in Germany, flying some of the special reconnaissance aircraft. Two aircraft from my unit were shot down over the USSR in 1958, a C-118 and a communications-intelligence C-130.[6]

Colleagues from the Pentagon, bent on such tasks as briefing Chancellor Konrad Adenauer and the King of Norway, would keep me informed. The Eisenhower administration viewed the Vanguard as a "stalking horse for the classified military reconnaissance satellites that were to follow. In July 1956, the first operational U-2 landed at my air base; friends accompanying the aircraft said that they were assigned to the 1st Weather Reconnaissance Squadron, a statement accompanied with a grin. My squadron flew support missions for them to bases like Adana in Turkey, Peshawar in Pakistan and Bodo in Norway.[7]

My wife, Jeanne, and I were on vacation in Valencia, Spain, on October 5, 1957, when we came down to breakfast in our hotel to find the headlines proclaim the orbiting of a Soviet satellite, a technological first. We could feel the dramatic change of attitude of Europeans toward Americans. The superman American who had contributed so much to World War II, who had furnished a generous Marshall Plan to resuscitate impoverished nations, who had produced hydrogen bombs, and other technological triumphs, was now inferior to the Soviets in the minds of many people. This mood was reflected in a chagrined America. Eisenhower signed a National Defense Education Act, authorizing huge sums of money to correct educational deficiencies. This act bolstered math, science, and foreign language training at all levels. Many people thought that Sputnik was evidence that the Russians had a superior school system which caused school children to stretch their intellectual capacities to the utmost.

A congressional committee, chaired by Senator Lyndon Johnson, worked with the President to expedite numerous programs, all in the name of national defense. In fact, the Soviets helped the United States program by flaunting their technological superiority. A cartoon in their *Krokodil* magazine showed golf-addict Eisenhower addressing his golf ball on a tee with, "Now go into orbit!" It was true that the first U.S. satellite, Explorer I, launched on January 31, 1958, was golf ball size compared to the Sputnik II, which carried a live dog. Explorer I found the Van Allen radiation belt, which caused great concern at first, until its properties were found to be less harmful than at first thought.

The U-2 aircraft flew twenty-seven successful missions from 1956 until one was shot down on May 1, 1960, disrupting a Khrushchev-Eisenhower conference. The resulting U-2 photographs soon showed no massive USSR buildup in their ICBM and bomber programs. In an attempt to quell interservice rivalry, development of the reconnaissance satellite was transferred for awhile to a research group, the Advanced Research Projects Agency (ARPA) in the Department of Defense. Subsequently, a reconnaissance satellite was launched in 1959, and the program began in earnest at the end of 1960.

Subsequently control of the reconnaissance satellite was transferred to the National Reconnaissance Office (NRO). The two major reasons why the photo reconnaissance satellite development was delayed for four years were: first, the success of the U-2 aircraft in locating and identifying targets for the Strategic Air Command, and second, the difficulty in selecting a booster to put the first U.S. satellite in orbit. The Army's Jupiter C, with strap-on rockets, won over the Navy Vanguard and the Air Force Atlas. The "missile gap" that President Kennedy bewailed in his 1960 campaign proved to not be as much of a threat as the intelligence community had concluded.

However, identifying Soviet ICBM sites was the first part of the problem. It was still necessary to provide navigational information to our ICBMs, which would guide them with sufficient accuracy to destroy a "hardened" target.

The most needed information was the location of the targets in relation to the ICBM launch point. An ICBM travels a parabolic arc, from launch site to target. Since the North American continent was tied to Europe with a single SHORAN measurement, a World Geodetic System was required, locating three axes points on a mathematical model for the Earth.

The second item needed was a mapping satellite, with special mapping cameras and photogram metric lenses for the required accuracy measurements.

Third, our ICBM's required precision-pointing accuracy and knowledge of gravity anomalies in the Earth's crust that could pull the ICBM off its pre-planned course. A collection program was initiated to collect these data.

President Johnson had followed this program closely ever since he chaired the Senate committee that was concerned with satellites. In a March 1967 speech at Nashville, he proudly reported on the success of the reconnaissance satellite. He said that the $35-40 billion dollars that the U.S. had spent on the program had resulted in information worth ten times as much. A couple of months later, as a representative of the Defense Intelligence Agency, I gave a speech on a related subject to the American Association of Geographers at Toronto, Canada. The main theme of the speech was that it was now possible to collect many types of geographic information and store it in a universal cartographic data base in such a way to easily provide such products as inventories of worldwide food crops, measurement of flood areas, and plant disease detection and control. A Canadian magazine asked permission to print the article. That the Soviets had a keen interest in the subject was evident a couple of years later when a CIA colleague asked me to evaluate an article that they had purchased from a Soviet source for $10,000. It was a copy of my 1967 Toronto speech, which was printed in the magazine!

Today, satellite intelligence collection is an accepted procedure, acknowledged by world leaders. Imaging techniques produce photographs capable of identifying small objects on the Earth's surface, define heat sources with infrared lenses, find metal with magnetic detectors, use radar to spot movements, and monitor maritime activity. Communications, including electronic emissions, are routinely intercepted and analyzed. An example of the improvement in performance of reconnaissance satellites is the comparison between the objectives stated in the 1954 development directive for a resolution of 50-foot objects by the television system from a 300-mile high orbit, to the current Keyhole cameras that can detect objects as small as six inches from a 150-mile high orbit.

Succeeding presidents cited the Open Skies Policy as an integral part of this nation's agenda; the most recent was by President George H. W. Bush during Desert Storm. It is now an agreed upon requirement for nations living together in peace through major arms agreements, such as the Conventional Forces in Europe Treaty, Strategic Arms Reduction Treaty, Intermediate-and Shorter-Range Nuclear Forces Treaty, Threshold Test Ban Treaty, Peaceful Nuclear

Explosion Treaty, three chemical weapons agreements, and the Open Skies Treaty.

In March 1992, twenty-six nations signed the Open Skies Treaty, which commits member nations in North America and Eurasia to open their airspace, on a reciprocal basis, to permit the overflight of their territory by unarmed observation aircraft. This is a breakthrough made possible because of the capabilities of both American and Russia satellites. The constellations of military satellites, now orbiting Earth, have a capability for photo reconnaissance, radar reconnaissance, signal intelligence, missile warning, military navigation and military communications. The orbiting reconnaissance platforms deter aggression by making it virtually impossible to hide military threats. The Open Skies policy can provide a model and a stepping stone during the formation of a new policy to help define the role that the U.S. will play internationally.

Notes

1. Michael Beschloss, *Mayday*, New York: Harper and Row, 1986, p. 78.
2. *Prologue: Quarterly of the National Archives and Records Administration*, Summer 1996, Vol. 28, No. 2.
3. Two books describing the aircraft development and capabilities are *Skunk Works* by Ben R. Rich and Leo Janos, New York: Little Brown & Co., 1994, and *Operation Overflight* by Francis Gary Powers, New York: Holt Rinehart & Wilson, 1970.
4. Michael Beschloss, op. cit., p.85.
5. Ben R. Rich, op. cit. Rich stated "to put an airplane in the sky in 8 months was a tremendous achievement." p. 132.
6. See Michael Beschloss, *Mayday*, op. cit.
7. Ben R. Rich, op. cit. p. 132.

Following the Sputnik crisis, NASA immediately began working on ways to achieve human spaceflight. In his 1961 speech, John F. Kennedy made clear his intentions to have a man on the Moon by 1970. NASA's first high-profile program was Project Mercury. This program served to determine whether or not humans were capable of surviving spaceflight. This was followed closely by Project Gemini, a program that was built upon the successes of Project Mercury and which utilized a two-man spacecraft. NASA's efforts for human spaceflight continued with Project Apollo, which fulfilled Kennedy's desire by putting humans on the lunar surface in 1969. Following the Skylab and Apollo-Soyuz Test Projects in the 1970s, NASA resumed its efforts for human spaceflight in 1981 with the Space Shuttle program. This program has allowed astronauts to service and repair satellites and to transport people, materials, and equipment to the International Space Station. —HH

"Building Blocks to Space"
by NASA Aerospace Technology Enterprise
NASAexplores.com, June 7, 2001

Rome wasn't built in a day, and neither was America's space program. It took decades of study and exploration to reach the point where astronauts and cosmonauts could live together in space for months at a time as they do now on the International Space Station (ISS). The building blocks to get to this point came in the form of four space campaigns: Mercury, Gemini, Apollo, and Space Shuttle. The whole "space race" concept was underscored in a 1961 speech where president John F. Kennedy declared America's resolve to land a human on the Moon by 1970.

The Mercury project was a series of six manned flights that extended beyond Earth's atmosphere, taking place from 1961 through 1963. Though the goal was to orbit the Earth, the first two flights merely went to sub-orbital altitudes beyond our atmosphere. While Mercury astronauts learned first-hand of many space travel challenges, the issues were limited by the reduced mobility the astronauts endured. They were strapped on their backs for the entire flight, which ranged from less than a half hour to just over a full day. Movement was highly restricted.

Mercury flights were launched with Titan and Redstone rockets, and the astronauts splashed down in small recovery capsules slowed by parachutes. Because the idea of space flight was so new and experimental, the process of getting up into space and back down onto Earth was a major undertaking in itself. Because it had never been done before, space vehicles had to be designed to overcome the intense heat that would come as the craft re-entered Earth's atmosphere. A lengthy debate ensued on the benefits of using a large, copper heat shield to diffuse the temperatures, versus ablation—the melting of a protective layer on the capsule—to safeguard the passengers. Ablation won, along with a change in design to create a blunt-ended capsule, which would better dissipate energy and heat.

The 10 manned flights of the Gemini flight program followed Mercury and extended from 1965 through 1966. Gemini built on the successes of Mercury, stressing the goals of subjecting men to long-duration flights, and docking with other orbiting objects. The longest Gemini flight lasted 10 days, and after several attempts, Gemini was able to dock and separate from Agena, an unmanned satellite. Astronauts participated in several extra vehicular activities (EVA), also called space walks.

Apollo's 11 manned missions brought heightened notoriety to the American space program, which had been [in] competition with Russia's corresponding agencies. In July 1969, an Apollo lunar lander became the first Earth craft to land a man on the Moon. While Apollo flights allowed humans greater mobility while in flight, astronauts were still strapped on their back in a small capsule for re-entry into Earth's atmosphere and splash down into an ocean for helicopter rescue. The Apollo craft consisted of three elements: the command module, the crew's quarters and flight control section, and spacecraft support systems. An Apollo command module was just a bit larger than a compact car. That's not that small until you consider that three men had to spend a week in those close quarters.

A part of the Apollo missions included the Skylab project, the first actual Space Station. Four teams of astronauts spent several days apiece onboard Skylab, an orbiting satellite, conducting numerous experiments that would have been impossible on Earth. In fact, just being on board Skylab was an experiment in itself. Skylab was launched in 1973 and was expected to stay in space for 10 years. An unstable orbit brought it to Earth in 1979.

Apollo flights also brought the Apollo/Soyuz missions of 1975. This was the first joint mission sponsored by two separate nations. The Russian and American flights launched from their corresponding countries, and docked to each other midflight. Apollo-Soyuz was much more than a foreign relations improver; it allowed for the exchange of information and technology from both nations and a spirit of cooperation that would continue for decades to come.

The current phase of space technology is the Space Shuttle program. Begun in 1981, there have been more than 100 Shuttle missions performed. One of Shuttle's biggest projects is the construction of the ISS by astronauts aboard the Shuttle.

Astronauts on the Space Shuttle have performed experiments, conducted EVAs, and researched the effects of microgravity on various life forms, including bacteria, plant life, and humans. The Shuttle orbiter fleet currently consists of five vehicles, all named for pioneering sea vessels: Atlantis, Columbia, Discovery, Endeavour, and Enterprise.

The Space Shuttle project still continues during construction of the ISS.

What lies ahead? The future is never laid out with certainty, but some good guesses are aboard Starship 2040, a full-sized mock-up of a commercial passenger spacecraft as it might look in the year 2040. Starship is housed in a 48-foot tractor-trailer rig and travels the country showing its exhibit to illustrate how future space travel will look. Some exhibits focus on propulsion technology, and others showcase the expected living conditions of space travel 40 years from now.

Courtesy of NASA.

In his State of the Union address before Congress in 1984, President Ronald Reagan made an Apollo-like announcement when he stated his plans to build a permanently inhabited space station. The progress made in completing this project has been the result of a collective effort from sixteen countries. Led by the United States' NASA, the team includes Canada, Japan, Brazil, Russia, and the European Space Agency (United Kingdom, France, Germany, Belgium, Italy, the Netherlands, Denmark, Norway, Spain, Switzerland, and Sweden). The assembly of the International Space Station (ISS) began in 1988

and is scheduled for completion in 2006. Since 2000, crews have lived in the station for months at a time, conducting experiments and continuing the construction. Upon its completion, the ISS will be able to house up to seven astronauts and will have six state-of-the-art laboratories. The ISS will be used mostly for scientific research in the unique environment of microgravity. In the microgravity environment of the ISS, scientists can explore phenomena that are masked by the gravity on Earth. It will allow new insights into things such as what happens inside a fire and how tumors grow. The International Space Station will also help scientists to learn valuable lessons that will prepare humans for long-term space exploration. —HH

"International Space Station"
by Stanley Holmes
Europe, March 1999

Last December 10, NASA astronaut Robert Cabana and Russian cosmonaut Sergei Krikalev swung open the hatch between the space shuttle *Endeavor* and the first element of the international space station, the Russian-built *Zarya* command module.

The historic moment was another example of international collaboration between the space agencies of Russia and the United States. But to reach that significant milestone, the two superpowers of space have drawn heavily on the resources and expertise of the sixteen nations involved in the largest scientific cooperative program in history.

While the Americans and the Russians have been in the spotlight with their rocket launches and space-walks, the Europeans have been quietly supplying both countries with computer hardware, technical expertise, and scientific equipment.

The role of the eleven European nations may not be as glamorous as the role of the Americans and the Russians, but it is no less significant. The success of the space station depends on a level of technical cooperation and scientific collaboration among the sixteen nations that has never before been attempted.

"We feel the internal cooperation is absolutely essential," said Michael O'Brian, deputy associate administrator for NASA. "Each of the partners is contributing something significant."

The Europeans are playing a leading role in promoting the international cooperation so vital to the success of the international space station. They see this project as a model for future global cooperative structures, reflecting European efforts over the past fifty years to unify the continent after engaging in two devastating world wars.

"In fifty years, we have turned our former enemies into friends," said Diter Isakeit, director of manned space flight for the European Space Agency (ESA). "We freely cooperate on many projects in Europe. We are on the leading edge of global cooperation. Now, we introduce that to the rest of the world."

Under the leadership of ESA, Belgium, Denmark, France, Germany, Italy, the Netherlands, Norway,

Spain, Sweden, Switzerland, and the United Kingdom are involved in all the key phases of the space station—from assembly and maintenance to scientific research in their own orbital laboratory.

The eleven European nations join the United States, Canada, Japan, Russia, and Brazil in one of the biggest nonmilitary joint efforts in history. The risky project is also as much about promoting peaceful cooperation in space exploration as it is about scientific and technological achievements.

The US space shuttle and two types of Russian rockets will conduct forty-five missions to launch and assemble the more than 100 elements that will comprise the completed international space station. In all, 460 tons of structures, modules, equipment and supplies will be placed in orbit by the year 2004.

The complex project involves more than 100,000 people at space agencies and hundreds of contractor and subcontractor companies around the world. Once completed, up to seven men and women will live and work on the permanent orbiting science and technology research base. They will conduct a diverse set of assignments, from life science and microgravity research to earth and space science experiments.

Europe's contribution includes the following:

- The *Columbus* laboratory is the entry ticket for Europe into the international space station as a full partner. It is a pressurized, habitable laboratory that will be carried to the space station by the space shuttle in

2003. *Columbus* will be the main work place for the scientific and technological activities of the European astronauts. Daimler-Chrysler Aerospace of Germany is the prime contractor, winning the largest single development contract ever placed by ESA.

- Aerospatiale of France is developing the automated transfer vehicle, a cargo-carrying upper stage for its *Ariane 5* rocket that can conduct automatic rendezvous and docking maneuvers with the space station. In addition to delivering up to nine tons of cargo to the station, the ATV can reboost the station into higher orbit and dispose of waste materials from the station. Waste materials are burned during the rocket's re-entry into the earth's atmosphere.

- ESA is cooperating with NASA on a prototype crew return vehicle, known as the X-38, which eventually will replace the Russian *Soyuz* spacecraft as an emergency crew return vehicle and accommodate up to six crew members.

- ESA is also developing early delivery elements for NASA and the Russian Space Agency. That includes laboratory support equipment for NASA valued at $69 million; an on-board computer system for the Russian service module worth about $59 million; and a European robotic arm, valued at $175 million, that will be used to assemble the Russian science and power platform.

- The Italian company Alenia Aerospazio is building two fully integrated nodes for the station. Europe also will supply cryogenic freezer racks, crew refrigerator freezer racks, engineering services for the early-delivery items, and computer hardware support for NASA's software development integration laboratory.

International cooperation, so far, has been one of the foundations of the space station's early success.

When the Russians were having financial troubles, the United States paid the difference to ensure the successful launch of the *Zarya* module.

"Each partner in such a complex project will have some difficulty," said O'Brian, of NASA. "What we've learned is that we can work together through these difficulties. It isn't easy, and it's usually financial, but through creative negotiations and goodwill, we have been able to find some solutions."

One creative solution involves the time-honored system of bartering among partners for high-tech equipment and laboratory or space shuttle time.

"Everything is bartered," Isakeit said. "We come back to old times. No government wants to finance high technology in another country. So, to cooperate, we exchange scientific equipment and other expertise."

All partners are responsible for their share of the costs to operate and use the space station. But partners can pay in cash or through "in-kind contributions." The Europeans have chosen barter arrangements to ease the costs as well as to send their astronauts on early space station missions. Technically, the Europeans can't use the space station until the arrival of the *Columbus* laboratory in 2003.

The Europeans developed the on-board computer system for the Russian service module. Instead of payment, the Russians gave the Europeans a docking station for their automated transport vehicle, Isakeit said.

In exchange for providing the laboratory support equipment to NASA, the European Space Agency plans to send scientists and astronauts to the US laboratory before the completion of the *Columbus* laboratory.

Through bartering arrangements with NASA, the Europeans also hope to send their astronauts on some early space station assembly missions.

"The people like to see our astronauts up in space," Isakeit said. "And we would like them to get the training and the practice."

Reprinted with permission from the Delegation of European Commission.

It has been more than a quarter of a century since the last manned spaceship has been developed in the United States. Since that time, not a single human has set foot on the Moon. As described in the following article from Astronomy, *President*

George W. Bush has crafted a policy that aims to change all of that. The policy proposes the use of advanced robots to assist humans in once again exploring the Moon and eventually traveling to Mars and beyond. Experiments conducted by NASA would focus on investigating how to sustain life in space and how to overcome obstacles that limit exploration. Unfortunately, the increase in spending that is necessary to send humans into space will undoubtedly lead to cutbacks in other NASA programs. Because of this, not all experts see eye-to-eye with the president. This article describes Bush's policy and the difficulties that he may face in getting Congress and the public to embrace it. —HH

"A New Vision for Space"
by Frank Sietzen Jr.
Astronomy, May 2004

Ironies crowded NASA's perilous year from February 2003 to February 2004, but one was astounding. An American president with no previous interest in space, along with a NASA administrator with no space-program experience, crafted a policy that space supporters had awaited for nearly four decades.

The nation's 43rd president proposed to return astronauts to the lunar surface within a decade and then prepare them for voyages to Mars and beyond. True space exploration—a human exploration agenda—would once again be the centerpiece of the U.S. civil space program.

And everything NASA does would fit that objective, or risk reduction or termination.

The new space policy had been rumored, whispered, and anticipated in Washington space circles for weeks. Now "spacers" had their hopes rewarded with the most ambitious human space-flight plan ever. It would send Americans into the solar system to explore the Moon, Mars, asteroids, and even farther. It would be space-faring in the classic tradition set more than four decades ago by another president, in another time of national uncertainty and testing.

Man to the Moon invokes an almost mythic resonance in the history of the late 20th century. The clarity of the goal set by President John F. Kennedy—man, Moon, decade—the ultimate success of the Apollo program, and the idea that the Moon-landing era was NASA's golden age have stood in contrast with all the space efforts that followed. By comparison, none of Kennedy's successors had successfully established humans to the Moon or Mars as a national goal. With enthusiasm for advanced space plans cooling, no substantial review of human space-flight goals had been undertaken in more than a decade and a half. But all that changed on January 14, 2004, with a new mandate from the Bush administration.

This initiative, which NASA calls Project Constellation, might be called "Mars by way of the Moon; robots and humans working together; developing exploration technologies." But not only are new program elements and vehicles central to achieving George W. Bush's goals; a thorough transformation of NASA itself will also be required. Adding to the new spacecraft, robots, and tools will be a subtraction of those elements of NASA that the agency will be required to give up— literally, to pay for the Moon.

First Finish What Was Started

To unveil his space-exploration initiative, Bush came to NASA's headquarters in Washington, the first time a sitting United States president had come to the agency's home. Space was important, Bush said: "It is a subject that's important to this administration, it's a subject that's mighty important to the country, and to the world." Noting it had been more than a quarter century since the last American human spaceship had been developed, the president pledged it was time to begin something new.

"In the past thirty years, no human being has set foot on another world, or ventured farther upward into space than 386 miles," a distance the president compared to a journey from Washington, D.C., to Boston. "It is time for America to take the next steps," he told the packed audience crowded into the agency's auditorium. "We will build new ships to carry man forward into the universe, to gain a new foothold on the Moon, and to prepare for new journeys to worlds beyond our own," Bush said. Why? "Because the desire to explore and understand is part of our character."

The future in space will begin with the two central elements of the existing U.S. manned space program: the space shuttle and the International Space Station (ISS). The top priority facing NASA is to return the shuttle to operations. Once flights resume, the shuttle will complete the orbital assembly of the International Space Station. "We will finish what we have started," Bush said, and once the station is completed, the fleet of three remaining shuttles will be retired, no later than 2010.

Beginning immediately, all research conducted by the United States using the station will shift to investigating how to sustain humans in space. "Research onboard the station and on Earth will help us better understand and overcome the obstacles that limit exploration," said the president. "Through these efforts, we will develop the skills and techniques necessary to sustain further space exploration."

Project Constellation

In addition, Bush's policy calls for the development of a new exploration-class human spacecraft called the Crew Exploration Vehicle, or CEV. "This will be the first spacecraft of its kind since the Apollo Command Nodule," the president explained. The CEV could make its first flight in 2008 and perform its first manned landing on the Moon by 2014. More substantial missions will follow, no later than 2020. The goal of the vehicles is to allow astronauts to live and work on the lunar surface for increasingly extended periods. Advanced robots will work with astronauts during their explorations of the Moon. This provides an incremental approach to lunar exploration. "We'll make steady progress—one mission, one voyage, one landing at a time," Bush said.

As with Apollo, robots will pave the way for human missions, with the first new robotic flights to the Moon starting about the same time as the CEV test flights,

2008. New power, propulsion, life support, and other systems that could sustain humans on other worlds will be tested during these lunar visits.

With technologies developed on the Moon, the United States will be ready for human missions to Mars—and worlds beyond.

Buying the Moon

Like the now-canceled Orbital Space Plane, the CEV will ride into space on an expendable launch vehicle, such as a Delta or Atlas or Ariane rocket. No new super-booster like Apollo's Saturn V is envisioned, although a cargo rocket using shuttle hardware is being studied. Industry, and possibly space entrepreneurs, may provide upper stages, space tugs, or propulsion modules.

When the new program was announced, NASA Administrator Sean O'Keefe was quick to say his agency hadn't decided on any specific configuration for the CEV. But many NASA sources say it will be almost certainly some form of space capsule, one version of which could serve as the Moon lander itself. Using existing vehicles and older, proven technology like capsules is aimed at keeping the development cost of the project low.

To pay for the initial steps of Project Constellation, Bush proposed to boost NASA's annual $15.5 billion budget by some $800 million next year, and 5 percent more each year for the next three years. Thereafter, the agency would get between 1 and 2 percent additional new funds a year, all devoted to Constellation. Much of the first installment of funding would go to begin development of the advanced robots. But more controversial is an additional $11 billion of existing agency funds that would be stripped from projects like the shuttle and other non-exploration research and redirected to Constellation.

Where all this money will come from, O'Keefe could not say. And after the next decade's research aboard the ISS, the United States will end its heavy use of the orbiting base, shifting focus to the Moon. Between the retirement of the shuttles and the birth of the CEV would lie a gap of two or three years, during which the United States will have no human space vehicle flying. The country will rely entirely on Russian Soyuz craft for lifts into space. By the time the Moon landings are underway, both of today's signature NASA projects, the shuttle and the station, will have ended.

Tough Sailing Ahead

The most difficult part of crafting a policy isn't the policy itself; it's what follows. Congress, and ultimately the public, must embrace it, a task that history indicates is almost as difficult to achieve as the missions themselves.

A review of the five previous attempts to set national space goals shows stunning achievement and failure. Twice, the efforts yielded the intended programs; twice, the proposals met with substantial revisions in Congress; and one effort failed completely. President Dwight Eisenhower initiated the first American manned space project (called Mercury) in 1959, following the establishment of NASA the previous October. Congress approved the Mercury program's objective of sending a man into space during the period from 1961 to 1963.

President Kennedy set a goal of landing humans on the Moon during an address to Congress on May 25, 1961. Congress funded the program, and six successful landings were achieved from 1969 to 1972. But public and political support cooled, and three remaining lunar landings, plus a follow-on program to expand the system into semi-permanent lunar bases, were canceled.

On January 5, 1972, President Richard Nixon initiated the reusable space-shuttle program to lower the cost of access to space. But budget cuts imposed from within the Nixon administration and Congress sharply reduced the shuttle from a fully reusable design to today's partly reusable one. That shift reduced short-term costs but led to a more expensive system to run. High operating costs plus delicate hardware have bedeviled the program all along. Instead of lowering launch costs, the shuttle became the most expensive launch vehicle ever, and its fragile design led to a pair of space-flight disasters.

More than a decade after Nixon authorized the shuttle program, another president proposed a new space plan. On January 25, 1984, President Ronald Reagan made building and launching a permanent space station the nation's civil space goal. But Reagan failed to defend the program from critics within his administration as well as from Congressional budget cuts. The station design was altered more than a dozen times while its cost soared from $8 billion to more than $100 billion. The redesigns delayed the completion of the station from "within a decade," as Reagan first sought, to the point where it's still under construction today.

President George H. W. Bush attempted launching his administration's own space goal in a speech on July 20, 1989, the 20th anniversary of the first Moon landing. The elder Bush proposed a program of manned lunar and Mars exploration. But lack of a consensus in his administration, as well as within NASA itself, doomed the plan. Congress failed to fund any element of the proposal, which ultimately was abandoned.

Now the younger George Bush has made his own effort at space planning. He will need to assemble a legislative coalition to start the project with a budget boost in 2005. Each year thereafter, new funding battles must be won to keep the project operating. Between now and the proposed first new landing on the Moon, three presidential elections will occur. Six Congresses will be elected. And the public, whose support will be crucial, will have ample opportunity to have its attention distracted by other issues, few of which can be anticipated today.

The political environment that greets President George W. Bush's space plan today is far different than that which faced John Kennedy's forty years ago. To succeed, Bush will need to forge a consensus not in space but on Earth, among groups that rarely agree on his other policies.

"We have a mandate," said NASA's O'Keefe less than an hour after Bush's announcement on January 14. That mandate is a challenge to achieve. But the hardest challenge of all will be translating it into hardware.

6

Bringing Space Technology Down to Earth

A map that not only shows the location of features on Earth but also their elevations is called a topographical map. Topographical maps are useful for just about any project that requires a detailed layout of the contours of the land. For many hard-to-reach areas, or areas with difficult terrain, topographical maps can be inaccurate or even nonexistent. The Shuttle Radar Topography Mission (SRTM) has alleviated this problem to a great extent. SRTM is a joint project of the National Geospatial-Intelligence Agency (NGA) and NASA. Using radar instruments to collect data from 80 percent of Earth's landmass, SRTM was able to create the most detailed, near global topographical map of Earth ever made. The following article from NASAexplores.com explains how the shuttle Endeavour was used to collect highly accurate topographical data and how this data benefits the military, civil, and scientific communities. —HH

"Mapping the Earth from Space"
by NASA
NASAexplores.com, September 6, 2001

Have you ever heard the phrase, "You can't see the forest for the trees"? Sometimes putting distance between objects helps things become clearer. That's the case when it comes to making maps of the Earth. Topographical maps—the maps that show changes in elevation—using images gathered by the Space Shuttle crew are providing a more detailed view of the world's terrain than have ever been gathered.

For 11 days in February 2000, the Shuttle Radar Topography Mission (SRTM) took pictures of Earth from on board Shuttle Endeavour mission STS-102. Close to a billion images were recorded and transformed into 3-dimensional (3-D) images that mapped over 80 percent of the Earth's surface. The images weren't taken with standard cameras, however. *Single-pass radar interferometry* is a process where radar beams are bounced off the Earth's surface and received by two antennae. One antenna was located in the Shuttle's payload bay, and the other was on a long, 200-foot (60.9-meter) mast. Layering the two separate radar images allowed for a more precise, 3-D view, much like your eyes would see. The Shuttle made over 150 orbits around Earth with radar mapping devices running constantly, taking a 200-kilometer (124-mile) wide swath of the surface below. These images were stored on video for later processing. Eighteen months later, the data was compiled into useful maps.

The images recorded on the SRTM mission are radar, not "regular" pictures that are easy to see on their own. Once recorded, engineers clarify blurry images, enhance lines, and overlay other satellite photos that depict roads and structures. The photos are shaded and colored to make them more distinguishable, and additional details such as trees are added in to help viewers recognize what they are seeing.

The 200-feet (60.9-meter) mast that held one of the radar cameras was the largest rigid structure ever deployed into space. A corkscrew design allowed the mast to unfold and extend into space, maintaining enough rigidity to stay in place, yet flexible enough to withstand the movements of the Shuttle.

"It was a very clever design for the mast," says Kevin Kregel, commander of STS-87. "The structure was enormous—the length of six city buses—yet somehow had to fit inside the Space Shuttle's cargo bay."

Kregel says that SRTM opened a new door to topographic mapping. Because images were recorded with radar, rather than standard cameras, the signals penetrated cloud layers and measured height to an accuracy of 3 to 15 meters (10 to 50 feet). "In the past, only 3 to 5 percent of the Earth was mapped to such a degree of accuracy," Kregel says. "Now we have 80 percent of the world recorded this precisely."

What are the uses of these detailed topographical maps? The National Imagery and Mapping Agency, an affiliate of the Department of Defense, sponsored the flight, so military uses are likely. Civilian applications could include helping find ideal locations for cell phone towers without sending people out to conduct field studies and for identifying habitats of endangered species. Airline pilots could supplement global positioning satellite readings to be better advised of natural hazards when flying. Perhaps the greatest advantage to the minute detail of SRTM's imaging benefits everyday people.

"Natural disasters happen everywhere," Kregel says. "Floods, snow storms, and droughts affect everyone. By knowing where the major flood plains are located, through these detailed topographical maps, dams can be built strategically to benefit the most people with the smallest risk. Rescue operations needed when disasters take place can now be conducted with the complete understanding of how the land is laid out. This particular use for SRTM information can save lives."

Courtesy of NASA.

Many of the advances in space technology that have been developed at NASA are finding their way into medicine. Scientists at NASA are working on ways to grow food on shuttles and in the International Space Station. The biggest

problem they face is growing plants without sunlight or soil. To solve the problem of a lack of sunlight, scientists are using light-emitting diodes, or LEDs, to provide the plants with light. Another technological advancement was developed by NASA to solve the question of how the nervous system adapts during space-flight. In an attempt to answer this question, scientists at NASA produced a software package called Reconstruction of Serial Sections (ROSS) that would allow them to visualize complex neural structures of the inner ear. What do these two NASA inventions have in common? They are both being used for the treatment of cancer. According to the CDC (Centers for Disease Control and Prevention), cancer is the second-leading cause of death in the United States. In the following article from the Washington Times, *the future of these technologies is discussed. —HH*

"NASA Research Aids Detection of Cancers"
by Amy Fagan
The Washington Times, December 28, 1997

Call it spinoffs from space. NASA technology is being adapted for diagnosis and treatment of cancer, and virtual-reality tools the space agency is developing will allow surgeons to rehearse complex operations.

Using software developed by NASA, physicians can get a three-dimensional view of breast tissue, allowing for a more accurate diagnosis of tumors.

And a special lighting technology originally developed for plant growth experiments in space may soon be used to treat brain cancer.

Photodynamic therapy uses tiny light-emitting diodes (LEDs) to activate light-sensitive, tumor-treating drugs. The light treatment appears to make the drugs more effective in destroying tumors. In the future, it may be used to treat children with inoperable brain tumors.

Experiments indicate that when special tumor-treating drugs are illuminated with LEDs, the tumors are more effectively destroyed than with conventional surgery, said Dr. Harry Whelan, pediatric neurologist at the Children's Hospital of Wisconsin and professor of neurology at the Medical College of Wisconsin.

NASA has funded contracts through the Small Business Innovation Research Program to demonstrate the feasibility of using LEDs in cancer treatment. The program is managed by the Technology Transfer Office at Marshall Space Flight Center in Huntsville, Ala. The LEDs were developed for Marshall Center by Quantum Devices Inc. of Barneveld, Wis., and the recent developments were announced in early November.

Dr. Whelan has obtained approval from the Food and Drug Administration to use the LED probe in the removal of brain tumors in children on a trial basis.

Dr. Whelan uses a drug called Photofrin 2, which is injected into the patient's bloodstream and attaches to tumorous tissue. It permeates the tumorous tissue, while leaving the other tissue unaffected. He then places the new LED probe near the affected tissue to eliminate the tumor and activate Photofrin 2. Once activated, the drug destroys the tumor's cells leaving the tender brain stem virtually untouched, he said.

The light source consists of 144 tiny diodes that form the tip of a neural probe about the size of a human finger, he said.

"This new probe illuminates through all nearby tissues," said Dr. Whelan. "We've used lasers before, but they are often unreliable and limited in color spectrum. Lasers are also very expensive and lose power."

The LED probe, however, can be used for hours at a time and remains cool to the touch. It can also be purchased at a fraction of the price of a laser, said a spokesman from Marshall Center.

"We are very happy to be a part of this innovative procedure," said Rose Allen, manager of the Space Product Development Office at the Marshall Center. "It's exciting to see how NASA's commercial space benefits results in benefits here on Earth. Who would have thought that experiments searching for ways to improve agricultural products would lead to a medical procedure that saves children's lives?"

LEDs were used as a low-energy light source on NASA's second U.S. Microgravity Laboratory Spacelab mission in October 1995. The purpose of the mission was to pursue opportunities for U.S. industry through the use of space.

Dr. Whelan anticipates full approval of what he says could be the "operating technique of the future."

"The LED technology developed by NASA offers new hope to children with cancer," he said. "Every one of our cases will be a critical case with no hopeful alternatives. We think this new probe will help give children with tumors a chance to live healthy, happy lives."

In recent weeks, Dr. Whelan has been contacted by several families of such children. He is currently working with 12 families nationwide.

Earlier this month, NASA presented technology that will help doctors diagnose breast cancer more easily.

Using Reconstruction of Serial Sections software (ROSS), combined with a patient's magnetic resonance imaging (MRI) breast scans, a three-dimensional image of the breast tissue is formed, said Dr. Muriel Ross of NASA's Ames Research Center in Moffett Field, Calif., which developed the ROSS technology.

The resulting "reconstruction" is a computerized object that a doctor wearing 3-D glasses can see clearly from all angles on a computer screen, she said.

The technology was presented at the Radiological Society of North America Conference in Chicago earlier this month.

Normally, mammograms are used for initial screening of breast cancer. If a suspicious lump is detected, a follow-up MRI can be conducted. Unfortunately, many times it is hard for a doctor to see where the tumor begins and ends, she said.

There are still some bugs to be worked out with the software, Dr. Ross said.

"For this initial reconstruction, we combined features of the ROSS software with another version of it used for CAT scans," Dr. Ross said. "Eventually, a special version will be developed just for the MRI. In the meantime, we have shown that high-fidelity 3-D reconstructions can be made from typical MRI breast scans."

The NASA Ames Center is also working in conjunction with Stanford University in Palo Alto, Calif., to establish a National Biocomputation Center devoted to exploring the use of virtual reality in medicine.

NASA has a long history of turning space technology into medical marvels. The following article from NASAexplores.com, an excellent site to learn about current and past NASA projects, gives several examples of what it refers to as "technology spin-offs." Equipment used in space is being used to detect breast cancer early, to take our temperatures in

seconds, and to help those with vision problems. It is also being used to detect osteoporosis and to record images of the organs in the human body. Materials used in space are also being used to deliver babies more safely and to provide those who have lost a limb with lighter, stronger, and less expensive prostheses. These are just a few of the examples of how space technology is benefiting us here on Earth today. In the future, NASA is certain to continue to develop exciting and beneficial products that impact our lives in profound ways. —HH

"Out-of-This-World Medical Marvels"
by NASA Human Exploration and Development of Space Enterprise
NASAexplores.com, April 11, 2002

When technology that helps humans work and live on the International Space Station also helps people on Earth live healthier lives, that's efficient use of tax dollars. When NASA developments are developed or adapted for commercial use, it's called a technology spin off. Several NASA spin offs have found their way to the medical community, and their original space-related use had little, if anything, to do with their current Earthly applications.

New materials were invented to create the X-33, an experimental vehicle for advanced space propulsion. A

185

composite material used in the X-33 is also part of a pair of "smart" forceps with embedded fiber optics. This material allows doctors to measure the amount of pressure being applied to an infant's head during delivery. The elasticity of the composite material will prevent the physician from exerting too great a force and possibly injuring the baby. These forceps will be used to train medical students before they actually work in a delivery room.

Digital image detectors developed by NASA for use in monitoring changes in the Earth's atmosphere are now being used for the early detection of breast cancer. The system captures sharper digital images while exposing the body to lower doses of radiation than with conventional mammography. The images can be digitally stored or sent with a computer.

Prosthetics—artificial body parts—improve the quality of life for many people on Earth. Until recently, the molds for making new arms and legs were made with plaster and corn starch materials that were heavy, fragile, and irreparable if damaged. A derivative of the foam insulation that covers the Space Shuttle external tank is lighter, stronger, and less expensive than the plaster used for prosthetics molds and works just as well as the original material. The new material saves costs and is able to be massproduced more efficiently.

Anyone who has been to the doctor's office is likely to have had his or her temperature taken with an ear probe. A hand-held thermometer takes a person's temperature in less than 2 seconds with a disposable probe that is inserted into the ear. This medical timesaver stems from NASA technology developed to measure the temperatures of stars and planets from Earth laboratories. Sensing a planet's infrared radiation works similarly to sensing a patient's body temperature.

NASA technology to process satellite images, along with technology for head-mounted vision enhancement systems for the International Space Station has been combined to help people with vision problems. A headset worn like goggles, three cameras, and a control unit will enhance images to correct the user's particular impairment. This technology, called Low Vision Enhancement System (LVES, pronounced Elvis) is not for the totally blind, but for those with low vision—partial sight that is not correctable by surgery or lenses.

A camera on a computer chip will help physicians track the onset of osteoporosis—thinning of the bones. By consolidating the various controls onto one chip, the device is small, lightweight, and uses a fraction of energy of multiple-chip cameras currently in use. For patients, this means smaller dosages of radiation and a lower cost. NASA initially developed the technology for recording images in space.

NASA has a long history of transferring technology to the medical community. Digital image processing, developed for Apollo Moon landings is now widely in use as computer-aided tomography—

CAT scans—that record images of organs in the human body. A heart repair procedure called balloon angioplasty uses low-temperature laser light carried through fiber optic bundles in a flexible catheter to unclog blood vessels. NASA pioneered this technology for remote sensing of Earth's ozone layer.

It's a small world!

Courtesy of NASA.

Separately, astronomy and genetics have done wonders in producing technological advances. Imagine what they can accomplish when combined. That is just what has been going on in the last few years. Maryland's Celera Genomics Group (which is involved in discovery and development of therapies for cancer, autoimmune diseases, and inflammatory diseases) and Purdue University, which is involved in wireless communications and military applications, have both benefited form this cross-pollination of technologies. The following article from Astronomy describes how technology swapping between scientists in the fields of astronomy and genetics has helped Purdue University's Center for Satellite Engineering to improve low-altitude communications and surveillance satellite systems and has provided

Celery Genomics with a faster way to deliver benefits to the public. In the future, it is likely we'll see more of such exchanges between sciences that were often seen as being very different from each other. —HH

"Astronomers Swap Secrets"
by W. B. Schomaker
Astronomy, **February 2002**

Although it's often difficult to understand what astronomers and geneticists really do behind closed observatory or laboratory doors, you can rest assured that it's more than simply gawking at faint, fuzzy smudges in the sky or torturing furry little animals for their DNA. As a matter of fact, today more than ever, we know that scientific endeavors regularly yield useful and practical technological advances. What's more, in the last few months, twin tales of collaboration and shared technology between astronomers and geneticists have underscored the potential of pure scientific research to affect our cyber-marinated lives.

In two independent (yet symbolically significant) events, computer codes designed to model the evolutionary concept of natural selection and software constructed to process the digital deluge of astronomical data from the Hubble Space Telescope (HST) have recently been swapped between astronomers and gene researchers.

Purdue University engineers, led by William Crossley of Purdue's school of Aeronautics and Astronautics and the Center for Satellite Engineering, employed "genetic algorithms" to construct a new, more efficient method for deploying and tracking low-altitude satellites used for wireless communications and military applications.

Meanwhile, Rockville, Maryland-based Celery Genomics Group recently licensed the rights to NASA's Operational Pipeline Unified Systems (OPUS) software, maintained by the Space Telescope Science Institute (STScI) in Baltimore.

For years, satellite engineers have attempted to improve low-altitude communications and surveillance satellite systems. So far the challenge has centered on clusters of three or more satellites, called constellations, and their ability to maintain contact with ground antennae for long periods of time. At present, satellites orbiting several hundred miles above Earth's surface lose contact with ground bases at least four times daily, constituting a total diurnal loss of about six hours.

Crossley and his colleagues report new findings that promise to reduce satellite communication blackouts by about two hours per day. Their research, published in the July/September issue of the *Journal of Astronautical Sciences*, uses computer algorithms based on Charles Darwin's concept of natural selection to choose the best orbital configuration of satellite constellations. The team fed hundreds of thousands of parameter combinations, including spacing between satellites, their heading, and height above Earth's surface, into their supercomputers. By allowing only the "best performing" solutions to survive, the algorithms continue to selectively iterate, yielding progressively better results.

The team was surprised to find that the best combination of orbital parameters was one that they hadn't really considered before. In all previous experiments, satellites were placed equidistant from one another. It turns out this need not be so. In fact, they found that the winning combination involves spacing two satellites very far apart and bringing in the third satellite very close to the rear of the second.

Celery Genomics, who recently completed the world's first assembled and annotated mouse genome, aims to use NASA's OPUS software in order to reduce the drain on their software engineering resources caused by the enormous volume of data gathered in genomics research. They feel that the recent licensing agreement with NASA will allow them to significantly reduce the time it takes to complete complex genomics projects, enabling a speedier delivery of potential benefits to the public sector.

Since the beginning of America's space program, technology that was originally

*designed to send us into space has also
served us well here on Earth. The Space
Technology Hall of Fame was designed to
honor those innovators who have quietly
transformed space technology into products
that save and improve lives here on Earth.
Since it began in 1988, the Space Technology
Hall of Fame has served both to give these
innovators their much-deserved recognition
and to increase public awareness of the benefits of space technology. There are many
technological advances that are deserving of
recognition. The following article from the
NASA Web site lists the 2004 inductees into
the Space Technology Hall of Fame. These
inductees include technologies used to correct
people's vision, to care for the chronically ill,
to help travelers and adventurers determine
their location precisely without the use of a
traditional map, and to help reduce consumer
costs for telecommunications. —HH*

"NASA Technologies Headed for the Space Technology Hall of Fame"
by Michael Braukus and Kevin Cook
NASA Web Site, February 25, 2004

The Space Foundation today announced the selection of
four "down to earth" technologies for induction into the
Space Technology Hall of Fame. Three were spawned by

NASA efforts, and the fourth by the work of the U.S. Air Force Research Laboratory.

The 2004 Hall of Fame winners range from a medical technology that enables thousands of people to see better to software able to determine satellite orbits with pinpoint accuracy.

The four products incorporating space-based technologies being inducted this year are LADARVision 4000 (LASIK eye surgery), the MedStar Medical/ Health Monitoring System, Precision GPS (Global Positioning System) Software System, and Multi-Junction (MJ) Space Solar Cells. Each brings to Earth a different life-enhancing benefit from space technology.

"For 16 years, the Space Foundation has honored extraordinary space technologies that enhance the quality of life on earth through its Space Technology Hall of Fame program," said NASA Administrator Sean O'Keefe. "The 2004 Hall of Fame honorees are a shining example of how the exploration of space returns incredible and sometimes unexpected benefits for all of us on earth."

Space Foundation President & Chief Executive Officer Elliot G. Pulham said, "Our 2004 honorees represent space technologies that save lives, enable thousands of people to see better, power modern global telecommunications and make travel safer for millions. They are great examples of why what we do in space matters on earth."

The inducted technologies and innovators will be honored at the 16th Space Technology Hall of Fame Dinner, to be held April 1 at the Broadmoor Hotel in

Colorado Springs, Colo. The awards dinner, co-sponsored by The Boeing Company, is the capstone event of the 20th National Space Symposium, March 29-April 1. Jim Albaugh, President & Chief Executive Officer, Boeing Integrated Defense Systems, will be the evening's corporate host.

The Space Foundation, in cooperation with NASA, established the Space Technology Hall of Fame in 1988 to honor the innovators who have transformed space technology into commercial products, to increase public awareness of the benefits of space technology, and to encourage further innovation.

The 2004 Space Technology Hall of Fame Inductees are:

LADARVision 4000: Fewer and fewer people now need eyeglasses or contact lenses thanks to laser vision correction surgery. Laser-Assisted In Situ Keratomileusis or LASIK is the most widely performed surgical procedure. It uses a laser and eye-tracking device to reshape the cornea and is based on technology used to assist spacecraft in delicate docking maneuvers. This enables LASIK to provide unmatched precision.

MedStar Monitoring System: The cost of caring for the chronically ill continues to grow. In-home care is part of the solution,

and statistics show significant patient health improvements through closer in-home monitoring. Cybernet's MedStar System allows health care professionals to remotely monitor patients, and evolved from research funded by NASA, the National Institute of Mental Health, and the Advanced Research Projects Agency. The research result was a miniature physiological monitoring device capable of collecting and analyzing a multitude of signals in real time, which also is used to monitor astronauts on the International Space Station.

Precision Global Positioning System (GPS) Software System: In 1985 NASA's Jet Propulsion Laboratory (JPL) began developing software to determine satellite orbits with pinpoint accuracy. This work led to the development of a sophisticated system that incorporates special GPS algorithms and now uses the Internet to deliver information enabling real-time positioning accurate to a few inches anywhere in the world for terrestrial users and for space-borne users in low Earth orbit. The Federal Aviation Administration has adopted JPL's software in their GPS-based navigation system to improve air travel safety for millions of travelers.

Multi-Junction (MJ) Space Solar Cells:
Responding to the need for higher efficiency
solar cells, the Air Force Research Laboratory
sponsored research and development efforts
to produce high efficiency multi-junction
space solar cells. MJ solar cell technology
provides a direct replacement for lower efficiency single-junction cells. The end results
are reduced space mission lifecycle costs,
reduced customer costs for telecommunica-
tion, weather forecasting and many other
services crucial to our daily lives on Earth.

Courtesy of NASA.

Web Sites

Due to the changing nature of Internet links, the Rosen Publishing Group, Inc., has developed an online list of Web sites related to the subject of this book. This site is updated regularly. Please use this link to access the list.

http://www.rosenlinks.com/cdfa/mmcse

For Further Reading

Benson, Michael. *Beyond: Visions of the Interplanetary Probes*. New York, NY: Abrams, 2003.

Chown, Marcus. *The Universe Next Door: The Making of Tomorrow's Science*. New York, NY: Oxford University Press, 2003.

Darling, David. *The Complete Book of Spaceflight: From Apollo 1 to Zero Gravity*. New York, NY: Wiley, 2002.

Kerrod, Robin. *Hubble: The Mirror on the Universe*. Buffalo, NY: Firefly, 2003.

Morton, Oliver. *Mapping Mars: Science, Imagination, and the Birth of a World*. New York, NY: Picador, 2002.

Preston, Richard. *First Light: The Search for the Edge of the Universe*. New York, NY: Random House, 1996.

Waller, William H., and Paul W. Hodge. *Galaxies and the Cosmic Frontier*. Cambridge, MA: Harvard University Press, 2003.

Bibliography

Anthes, Gary H. "University of California, Berkeley Scientists Develop Algorithms to Discover Extra-Solar Planets." *Computerworld,* Vol. 36, No. 23, June 3, 2002, pp. 28–29.

Berger, Daniel. "The Failure of Theory: Models of the Solar System." *National Forum,* Vol. 81, No. 1, Winter 2001, pp. 6–7.

Braukus, Michael, and Kevin Cook. "NASA Technologies Headed for the Space Technology Hall of Fame." NASA. February 25, 2004. Retrieved September 24, 2004 (http://www1. nasa.gov/lb/home/hqnews/2004/feb/ HQ_04069_hall_ of_fame.html).

Britt, Robert Roy. "Universe 156 Billion Light-Years Wide." Space.com., May 24, 2004. Retrieved September 24, 2004 (http://www.space.com/ scienceastronomy/mystery_monday_040524.html.

Cowen, Ron. "Modeling the Whole Universe." *Science News,* Vol. 154, No. 1, July 4, 1998, p. 11.

Croswell, Ken. "Light-Years Ahead." *Sky and Telescope*, Vol. 89, No. 4, April 1995, pp. 6–7.

de Grasse Tyson, Neil. "On Earth as in the Heavens." *Natural History*, Vol. 109, No. 9, November 2000, pp. 90–92.

Fagan, Amy. "NASA Research Aids Detection of Cancers." *Washington Times*, December 28, 1997, p. 8.

Gibbons, Ann. "Putting Einstein to the Test—In Space." *Science*, Vol. 254, No. 5034, November 15, 1991, pp. 939–941.

Higgins, Thomas V. "Telescopes: All Eyes on the Skies." *Laser Focus World*, Vol. 31, No. 2, February 1995, pp. 63–69.

Holmes, Stanley. "International Space Station." *Europe*, No. 384, March 1999, pp. 16–18.

Leary, Warren E. "The Cosmos Gets Another Set of Eyes." *New York Times*, April 8, 2003, Section F.

Lemonick, Michael D. "Beyond Hubble." *Time*, Vol. 156, No. 20, November 13, 2000, pp. 84–88.

Mac Low, Mordecai-Mark. "The Virtual Universe." *Natural History*, Vol. 109, No. 1, February 2000, pp. 88–92.

Max Planck Society. "Computer Simulations Predict What Astronomers Will 'See' with Gravitational Wave Telescopes When Two Black Holes Collide." *Science Daily*, September 19, 2001. Retrieved July 27, 2004 (http://www.sciencedaily.com/releases/2001/09/010919074007.htm).

Monastersky, Richard. "The Venus Hunters." *Chronicle of Higher Education*, Vol. 50, No. 36, May 14, 2004, p. A16.

Bibliography

NASA. "Mapping the Earth from Space." September 6, 2001. Retrieved July 27, 2004 (http://www.nasaexplores.com/show2_912a.php?id = 01-056&gl = 912).

NASA. "NASA Gravity Probe B Mission Enters Science Phase, Ready to Test Einstein's Theory." September 7, 2004 (http://www.msfc.nasa.gov/news/news/releases/2004/04-228.html).

NASA Aerospace Technology Enterprise. "Building Blocks to Space." June 7, 2001. Retrieved July 27, 2004 (http://www.nasaexplores.com/show2_articlea.php?id = 01-043).

NASA Human Exploration and Development of Space Enterprise. "Out-of-This-World Medical Marvels." April 11, 2002. Retrieved July 27, 2004 (http://www.nasaexplores.com/show2_articlea.php?id = 02-030).

Pool, Robert. "Closing In on Einstein's Special Relativity Theory." *Science*, Vol. 250, No. 4985, November 30, 1990, pp. 1207–1208.

Rentmeester, Lester F. "Open Skies Policy and the Origin of the U.S. Space Program." *Air Power History*, Vol. 51, No. 2, Summer 2004, pp. 38–45.

Schomaker, W. B. "Astronomers Swap Secrets." *Astronomy*, Vol. 30, No. 2, February 2002, pp. 22–23.

Sietzen, Frank, Jr. "A New Vision for Space." *Astronomy*, Vol. 32, No. 5, May 2004, pp. 48–51.

Simcoe, Robert A. "The Cosmic Web." *American Scientist*, Vol. 92, No. 1, January-February 2004, pp. 30–37.

Stevens, Scott. "Reach for the Stars." *Communications News*, Vol. 36, No. 12, December 1999, pp. 78–79.

Talcott, Richard. "Edge of the Solar System." *Astronomy*, Vol. 29, No. 3, March 2001, p. 32.

Index

About the Editor

Heather Elizabeth Hasan graduated from college summa cum laude with a dual major in biochemistry and chemistry. She lives in Greencastle, Pennsylvania, with her husband, Omar, and their son, Samuel.

Photo Credits

Front cover (top inset) © Royalty-Free/Corbis; (center left inset) © Digital Vision/Getty Images; (bottom right inset) © NASA and Hubble Heritage Team (AURA/STScl); (bottom left inset) © Library of Congress Prints and Photographs Division; (background) Brand X Pictures/Getty Images. Back cover (top) © Photodisc Green/Getty Images; (bottom) © Digital Vision/Getty Images.

Designer: Geri Fletcher; Series Editor: Brian Belval